# 臥虎藏龍

# CROUCHING TIGER, HIDDEN DRAGON

## PORTRAIT OF THE ANG LEE FILM

FOREWORD AND NOTES BY
Ang Lee and James Schamus

INTRODUCTIONS BY
Richard Corliss and David Bordwell

SCREENPLAY BY
Wang Hui Ling, James Schamus, Tsai Kuo Jung,
based on the novel by Wang Du Lu

PHOTOGRAPHS BY
Chan Kam Chuen

A NEWMARKET PICTORIAL MOVIEBOOK

NEWMARKET PRESS
NEW YORK

Edited by Linda Sunshine
Designed by Timothy Shaner

All production photographs by Chan Kam Chuen.

This book is published simultaneously in the United States of America and in Canada.

First Edition

00  01  02  10  9  8  7  6  5  4  3  2  1

ISBN 1-55704-459-7 hardcover
ISBN 1-55704-457-0 paperback

Library of Congress Cataloging-in-Publication Data is available upon request.

QUANTITY PURCHASES
Companies, professional groups, clubs, and other organizations may qualify for special
terms when ordering quantities of this title. For information, write Special Sales,
Newmarket Press, 18 East 48th Street, New York, New York 10017; call (212) 832-3575;
fax (212) 832-3629; or email: sales@newmarketpress.com.
www.newmarketpress.com

Manufactured in the United States of America

Other Newmarket Pictorial Moviebooks include:
*Gladiator: The Making of the Ridley Scott Epic*
*Titus: The Illustrated Screenplay*
*The Age of Innocence: A Portrait of the Film*
*Cradle Will Rock: The Movie and the Moment*
*The Sense and Sensibility Screenplay and Diaries*
*Saving Private Ryan: The Men, The Mission, The Movie*
*Amistad: A Celebration of the Film by Steven Spielberg*
*Bram Stoker's Dracula: The Film and the Legend*

# CONTENTS

開鏡大吉

影片　臥虎藏龍

導演　李安

製片　江志強
　　　徐立功
　　　崔宝珠

# By ANG LEE

洪

The film is a kind of dream of China, a China that probably never existed, except in my boyhood fantasies in Taiwan. Of course, my childhood imagination was fired by the martial arts movies I grew up with and by the novels of romance and derring-do I read instead of doing my homework. That these two kinds of dreaming should come together now, in a film I was able to make in China, is a happy irony for me.

My team and I chose the most populist, if not popular, genre in film history—the Hong Kong martial arts film—to tell our story, and we used this pop genre almost as a kind of research instrument to explore the legacy of classical Chinese culture. We embraced the most mass of art forms and mixed it with the highest—the secret martial arts as passed down over time in the great Taoist schools of training and thought.

What is the Tao, the "way?" Of course, if you can say it, it's not the real Tao. It's enigmatic, in that it can only manifest itself through contradictions, through the conflicts of the heart rather than through the harmony it seeks. At least that was my experience of the Tao while making the movie! For example, the martial arts film is very masculine, but in the end our film finds its center in its women characters. It is the women who, in the end, are walking the path of the "way."

Another conflict was how to maintain a balance between the drama and the martial arts in the film. The film is not crafted in the realistic style, as my earlier films have been, but the emotions it conveys are real. So you will see that the drama is itself choreographed as a kind of martial art, while the fighting is never just kicking and punching, but is also a way for the characters to express their unique situation and feelings. At the same time, working with martial arts master Yuen Wo Ping and his team allowed me to learn an abstract form of filmmaking, where the images and editing are like dance and music.

It was a tremendous privilege for me to make this movie.

LEFT: *Ang Lee, his wife, and two sons join the cast and crew in the Xinjiang desert for a Good Luck Ceremony on the first day of shooting. Performed at the start of every Ang Lee movie, the tradition is meant to show respect.*

# MARTIAL MASTERPIECE

氣

## By RICHARD CORLISS

Consider for a moment the cinematic and emotional vectors converging in Ang Lee's *Crouching Tiger, Hidden Dragon*. A $15 million action movie and a poignant tragic romance. A fight choreographer, Yuen Wo Ping, who had won international acclaim for his work on *The Matrix* and was bound to tangle with the soft-spoken, hard-to-budge Lee. A topflight, all-Asian cast, with Chow Yun Fat (Hong Kong), Michelle Yeoh (Malaysia), Zhang Ziyi (Beijing), and Chang Chen (Taiwan). Only one of the cast—Zhang, then a 19-year-old ingenue—spoke anything like the mainland Mandarin that Lee demanded. At least these dangers were built into the scenario. What no one expected was that Yeoh would break her knee and need a month's rehab, or that it

*As the sage said:*

*Dying is easy, filmmaking*

*is hard.*

*Director Ang Lee and actress Zhang Ziyi (Jen).*

would rain sheets in the Gobi.

As the sage said: Dying is easy, filmmaking is hard. But everyone was so serious on *Crouching Tiger* because Lee, who made his reputation with adult dramas-of-manners like *The Wedding Banquet* and *Sense and Sensibility*, had a child inside screaming to get out. He was finally ready to pay homage to his lifelong ardor for martial-arts novels and pictures. He had made

beautiful films; now he would bend his considerable artistry to make, dammit, a movie. And nothing only about it.

Now that *Crouching Tiger* has opened, after stoking enthrallment at this May's Cannes Festival, viewers can see that all the agony produced exactly what Lee hoped to create: a blending, not a collision, of Eastern physical grace and Western intensity of performance, of Hong Kong kung-fu directness and British attention to behavioral nuance. Chinese stars convene from three movie eras: pioneer kung-femme Cheng Pei Pei from the '60s, Chow and Yeoh from Hong Kong's glorious '80s, and bright new lights Zhang and Chang. The fight scenes evoke grand old movies with computer technology. It's contemplative, and it kicks ass. High art meets high spirits on the trampoline of the movie's plot. Lee initially described the film to Yeoh as *"Sense and Sensibility with martial arts."* But it's not a hybrid; it's a new, exotic strain. Put it this way: a powerful film, a terrific movie.

Based on part of a Wang Du Lu novel that runs to several volumes and thousands of pages, the script by James Schamus, Wang Hui Ling, and Tsai Kuo Jung concerns the theft of a sword, the Green Destiny. This is the holy weapon of Li Mu Bai (Chow), a noble and expert warrior looking for peace in his later days. He entrusts the sword to Yu Shu Lien (Yeoh), a gifted martial artist with whom he shares an unspoken love. Then Jen (Zhang), daughter of a political bigwig, arrives, and everything tips off-balance. The wiser, more cautious adults are both drawn to and upset by Jen's beauty and vagrant energy. They sense Jen's avidity for

rare toys like the Green Destiny. They are also suspicious of her governess (Cheng Pei Pei), who bears a resemblance to Jade Fox, a ruthless thief and the killer of Li Mu Bai's master. And then one night, the sword disappears.

The Green Destiny is what Hitchcock called the MacGuffin: the object that kick-starts the adventure and puts everyone in frantic, purposeful motion. In *Crouching Tiger*, that motion has its own poetry; for these semi-gods and demidevils have a buoyancy to match their gravity. The film's first action scene, with Shu Lien chasing the sword's thief (who, we soon learn, is Jen), sets the tone and the rules. The two fight hand-to-hand and foot-to-foot, with elbows at the ready. Jen suddenly floats up, as if on the helium of her young arrogance,

and cantors up and down the courtyard walls as if they were velvet carpets, with Shu Lien in graceful pursuit. Jen executes a squat spin, then rises like a vertical dervish and escapes.

At its screenings in Cannes, this scene was greeted with spontaneous applause, even from those professional misanthropes, the critics. From that moment on, *Crouching Tiger* had the Riviera swells in its pocket. They gasped with glee as Jen and Jade Fox soared into the night (Who does that? Angels and witches.) They misted up at the friendship of Mu Bai and Shu Lien, two brave warriors who haven't quite the courage to say I love you. They happily took the film's 20-minute detour to the Gobi, where in a flashback Jen meets her bandit beau Lo (Chang) and makes love with the

*The Green Destiny is what Hitchcock*

*called the MacGuffin: the object that*

*kick-starts the adventure and puts*

*everyone in frantic, purposeful motion.*

spontaneity of a first-time tryst and the calculation of a girl who has to be on top. (Forget the tepid marriage her father has arranged. Jen wants to love a fighter and fight her lover.) At the end, they sobbed farewell to an old friend who gives a beautiful valediction.

Ang Lee does not like to compromise, but he has to adapt. He had first thought of Jet Li, he of the flying feet and dour demeanor, as Li Mu Bai. When Chow took the role, the action scenes were reduced but the character ripened. And, at times, what seems like a disappointment can be a sweet surprise. That was the revelation of Zhang Ziyi.

For all its pan-Asian star power, the movie depends on Jen and the actress who plays her. When first seen, Jen seems lovely but unformed, a dreamy adventuress who wants the

*Ang Lee and Chow Yun Fat (Li Mu Bai).*

freedom of the heroes she reads about. In one sense, she's the spoiled rich girl with a racing emotional motor. She aches for the forbidden thrill because she knows she would like it—and knows she'd be good at it. Gradually, though, Jen (or, rather, Zhang) reveals the steel will beneath her silky ways—and a more toxic, intoxicating beauty. On the cusp of womanhood, she could tumble either way: become a fearless heroine or a ferocious harlot. We know that she is guilty of one theft: She steals the film.

Everything is pretty in movies, but nothing is easy. And that includes Zhang's immersion into the character. She got to know the actor who would play her demon lover because, as Chang says, "We took acting lessons before we started the parts, so we were familiar with each other before shooting started." Lee's pre-production

instructions to the young actor were simple: eat. "My biggest task was to put on weight, as the director said I was too skinny." (He bulked up fine; he's halfway to hunkdom.)

But Lee had stricter demands of his starlet. "For a time," he says, "she was nowhere near where I thought Jen should be. But when you can't get something to work, you improvise. If the mountain doesn't turn around, make the road turn around. So we made the character closer to her until there was a meeting in the middle. We veered the movie toward her. She is very sexy and we thought, sure, let's use that. It makes things start to happen. She is the most marvellous thing I've found."

Zhang Ziyi, though a game gal, was not schooled in martial arts, so lithe young stunt doubles, male and female, executed the more strenuous feats. "In

China they say to find a good stunt-woman," Lee says, "is harder than finding a good wife." And to find a woman who is tops in stuntwork, acting, and all-round allure is almost impossible. That's why Yeoh is so precious. On one good leg or two, she wore those wires, scaled those walls.

"I've waited 15 years to work with this guy," says Yeoh, who signed on early and accompanied Lee on some location scouting. "He's gentle and very emotional. During a sad scene at the end of the film, he kept telling me to do different things, and when he'd come over I saw he was red-eyed, teary. I could barely look at him. He gets so completely involved. And when he says, 'Good take,' after a shot, he really means it." For Lee, that was a great take. "I know those weren't 'acting' tears, they were real tears. It works, and it brought tears to my eyes. Michelle had

to cry in every take, for five hours. At the end she was drained."

After two Hollywood tough-guy films and a lovely turn as the King of Siam in *Anna and the King*, Chow was used to learning a new language with each script: "First English, then Thai, now this." But the experience was, as he says, "awful. The first day I had to do 28 takes just because of the language. That's never happened before in my life. It gave me a lot of pressure."

So Chang and Zhang went to acting school; Chow and Yeoh crammed to speak Mandarin. And throughout, Lee was learning the limitations in the laws of stunt physics from Yuen. Movies, like life, are an education on the fly, with pop quizzes every moment. How apt, then, that the theme of *Crouching Tiger* should be teaching. In this war of the generations, the adults are as eager to

instruct the young as the kids are to rebel against authority. And the wicked carry grievances for years. Jade Fox says she killed Mu Bai's master because "he would sleep with me but never teach me" the secrets of *wuxia*; and she bitterly resents Jen because the child hoarded martial lore for herself. Here, knowledge is power. And only the most powerful, like Mu Bai, can share it.

The star pupil, of course, is Jen, and the film's main question is: From whom will she agree to learn? Shu Lien and Mu Bai both want to test themselves against her precocity. But for Mu Bai it is a mission. "What do you want?" Jen asks him, and he replies, "What I've always wanted—to teach you." For him education is a kind of intellectual and ethical parenting. Teaching this bright, willful girl is as close as he will come to fatherhood—

even if, as he must be aware, the job carries fatal risks.

"She needs direction and training," Mu Bai says of Jen. Surely that is Ang Lee speaking. A film director is the ultimate father figure, doling out responsibility, praise, and censure. On *Crouching Tiger*, Lee, who secured his early fame with the so-called "Father Knows Best" trilogy (*Pushing Hands, The Wedding Banquet, Eat Drink Man Woman*), was a father-teacher to Zhang the budding actress, to Yeoh the first-year Mandarin student, to Chow the man on the flying bamboo. And behind Lee was another family figure: the young Ang, mesmerized by tales of great fighters and images of impossible physical grace.

—RICHARD CORLISS
*Time* Magazine film critic

# HONG KONG MARTIAL ARTS CINEMA

## By DAVID BORDWELL

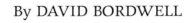

The *wuxia pian*, or film of martial chivalry, is rooted in a mythical China, but it has always reinvented itself for each age. Like the American Western, the genre has been reworked to keep in touch with audiences' changing tastes and to take advantage of new filmmaking technology. Yet at the center it retains common themes and visceral appeals.

In Japan, only members of the samurai class could carry a sword, but in ancient China both aristocrats and commoners could become professional swordsmen. Since the land was ruled by rival warlords, an unattached fighter could become a killer for hire. This sordid reality became glamorized in the *wuxia* tales that became popular after the ninth century AD. Like the Arthurian legends of Europe, the *wuxia*

promoted a conception of knightly virtue. The roaming hero was not only strong and skillful; he or she also had an obligation to right wrongs, especially when the situation seemed dire. The hero fought for *yi*, or righteousness—not for rights in the abstract, or for society as a whole, but for fairness in a particular situation—usually seeking retribution for a past wrong.

Here political history becomes crucial. China has had an unhappy history of corrupt and tyrannical regimes, dislodged only by court intrigue and assassination. Since civil society could not guarantee the rule of law, the *wuxia* knight-errant became the central hero of popular imagination. He or she was an outlaw who could deliver vengeance in a society where law held no sway. The

15

*The roaming hero was not*

*only strong and skillful; he or she also*

*had an obligation*

*to right wrongs.*

revenge motive took on moral resonance through the Confucian scale of obligations: The child owes a duty to the father, the pupil to the teacher. The *wuxia* plot often presents a struggle between social loyalty and personal desires, as when in *Crouching Tiger, Hidden Dragon,* Li Mu Bai's final mission to avenge the death of his teacher prevents him from simply retiring from the Giang Hu world to live with Shu Lien.

*Wuxia* characters and plots entered Peking Opera in the nineteenth century, where dazzling acrobatics added to their impact. *Wuxia* novels, often serialized in newspapers and running to hundreds of pages, became mass literature in Shanghai shortly thereafter. As Chinese filmmaking emerged in the 1920s, screenwriters drew stories from martial arts plays

and novels, building scripts around both male and female adventurers. (Most Westerners are surprised to find how central women warriors are in the *wuxia* tradition.) The epic Shanghai film *Burning of the Red Lotus Monastery* (1928), released in eighteen parts, became a progenitor of the fantasy film. Using flying daggers and wirework, it employed over 300 martial artists. The genre grew during the interwar years, both on the mainland and among the emigré companies of Hong Kong. When Mao's 1949 revolution dictated new cinema policies, Hong Kong and Taiwan held a monopoly on *wuxia* filmmaking.

To serve Hong Kong's large Asian market, films were made in both Cantonese (the local Chinese dialect) and Mandarin (the more widely spoken dialect). Cantonese *wuxia pian* of the

1950s and early 1960s emphasized magic and fantasy. Warriors soared endlessly, swords and daggers turned to fire, and fighters' hands could emit jagged bolts of lightning to stun their opponents ("palm power"). The plots were sketchy and the special effects were crude (sometimes scratched directly on the film negative), but the supernatural films established some permanent techniques of the genre. Reverse-motion shooting created impossible stunts, like leaping onto a roof. Hidden trampolines launched fighters into the air, and strong wires kept them aloft. On the soundtrack, thunderous whooshes underscored leaps and blows.

In reaction to the Cantonese fantasy films there emerged the "new *wuxia pian,*" a school of more realistic swordplay films influenced by

Japanese movies and a younger generation of martial arts novelists. Filmed in Mandarin and produced by big studios like Shaw Brothers, these tales didn't shy away from giving their warriors astonishing abilities, but the supernatural aura vanished. Now feats were presented as things which could be executed by a very disciplined fighter. In *The Jade Bow* (1966), the hero and heroine pursue ninja-like assassins over rooftops with a fluidity that seems only a slight exaggeration of natural human grace. Women warriors remained central to the tradition, but now they were given opportunities to contrast their styles with men's. Cheng Pei Pei became famous and known as the "Queen of *wuxia pian*" for her roles in *Come Drink with Me* (1966) and *Golden Swallow* (1968). In *Fourteen Amazons* (1972), when an army's generals are

massacred, their widows take up arms to avenge them in spectacular combat sequences.

The Mandarin *wuxia pian* also intensified realism by focusing not on aristocrats but on commoners, tormented heroes and heroines driven by ambition or revenge or devotion to justice and undergoing extreme physical suffering. Zhang Che quickly built a reputation for his sadomasochistic swordplay dramas, emblematized in his *One-Armed Swordsman* (1967) and *New One-Armed Swordsman* (1971). In contrast were the delicate, lyrical masterworks of King Hu. Hu brought the energy and finesse of classical Chinese theater and painting to the new swordplay movies. His films lingered on breathtaking landscapes, treated swordfights as airborne ballets, and created a gallery of reserved,

preternaturally calm warriors who fought not for prestige or vengeance but to preserve humane values. Perhaps the most famous scene in all the new *wuxia pian* comes midway through Hu's *A Touch of Zen* (1971), where combat unfolds in a quiet bamboo grove. Although fighters clash in midair, hurling themselves from spindly branches high above the ground or dive-bombing one another in a flurry of fast cuts, the overall impression is of poise—the sheer serenity of perfectly judged physical movement.

Swordplay films fell out of favor in the mid-1970s as kung-fu swept the world and gave the Hong Kong film industry a cheaper genre to exploit. Still, there were efforts to revive the *wuxia pian*. Patrick Tam's brooding *The Sword* (1980) reflected Japanese

influence. Action choreographer Ching Siu-tung turned to directing, and created a supple, modern flying swordplay style in *Duel to the Death* (1982). At a less spectacular level, the great Shaws' kung-fu director Lau Kar-leung turned to *wuxia* swordplay in his comedy *Shaolin vs. Ninja* (1978) and especially in *Legendary Weapons of China* (1982), a virtual anthology of *wuxia* devices, both magical (a magician controls a fighter from a distance by manipulating a doll) and historical (the final fight scene displays over a dozen weapons and fighting techniques).

Above all, it was producer-director Tsui Hark who spearheaded the revival of all manner of *wuxia*. Tsui's first film, *The Butterfly Murders* (1979), enhanced swordplay with futuristic weaponry, and he went on to revive fantasy swordplay in his dazzling, flamboyant

*Zu: Warriors from the Magic Mountain* (1983), for which he imported Hollywood special-effects experts. He went on to team with Ching Siu-Tung for the trailblazing *Chinese Ghost Story* (1987), which melded supernatural swordplay, horror, comedy, and romance. With its bisexual ghost and animated skeletons, *A Chinese Ghost Story* triggered a fashion for flamboyant, almost campy swordplay fantasies. Tsui knew a good thing when he saw it. His productions *The Swordsman I* (1990) and *Swordsman II: The East Is Red* (1992), *Green Snake* (1993), and other hits relied on gender-bending transformations, outrageous aerobatics, thundering music, and stunning set designs. They also showcased Brigitte Lin, Jet Li, Joey Wang, Maggie Cheung, and other popular stars of the period.

Like all Hong Kong cycles, the updated fantasy *wuxia* wound down, and a new trend surfaced. Under Tsui's auspices Yuen Wo Ping, one of the great kung-fu choreographers and directors, made *Iron Monkey* (1993), a mixture of kung-fu and swordplay that was also grounded in the reality of traditional techniques. Daniel Lee's fascinating *What Price Survival?* (1994) featured classic *wuxia* performers in an enigmatic tale pitting Japanese and Chinese swordsmen against one another. Tsui himself revisited the 1960s' grittier *wuxia pian* tradition in *The Blade* (1995), a savage and tumultuous tale in which a one-armed swordsman avenges his wounding and his father's death. Most important was Wong Kar-wai's *Ashes of Time* (1994), told in laconic dialogues over wine, splintered flashbacks, and strobe-pulsed fight scenes, all awash in a melancholic score. *Ashes* offers a poetic meditation on the *wuxia* tradition itself, as old fighters brood over their wasted lives, mourning the youth and loves they have lost.

From a historical perspective, *Crouching Tiger, Hidden Dragon* becomes a millennial synthesis of the great *wuxia* tradition. Based on a *wuxia* novel from the interwar period, its story of two generations recapitulates elements from the greatest of the Chinese swordplay films. The serene self-possession of Li Mu Bai is reminiscent of King Hu's fighters, and his decision to give up his Green Destiny sword becomes a solemn acceptance of the wastefulness of killing. Still, he cannot foreswear the need to avenge the death of his master, and so he launches a new cycle of pursuit and suffering. Yu Shu

Lien's rooftop pursuit of the mysterious thief echoes 1960s' adventures, and her unfussy prowess puts her in the line of women warriors played by Wu Lizhen, Josephine Siao Fong-fong, and Cheng Pei Pei. Cheng herself is on hand as a witness to the golden age, playing Jade Fox, the vengeance-mad swords-woman. The young couple, Jen and Lo, recall the combative couples of *Shaolin vs. Ninja*; by the end, however, their love affair, told through sumptuous desert flashbacks, acquires a sweeping poetic anguish akin to that of *Ashes of Time*. Behind the scenes is choreographer Yuen Wo Ping, a living encyclopedia of Peking Opera, martial arts techniques, and cinematic fireworks. In Yuen the sheer energetic physicality of the *wuxia* tradition has found one of its masters: The purpose, he explains, is "to make the viewer feel the blow."

Blending everything is Ang Lee, fully aware of the landmarks of the genre he's working in, and like his predecessors he at once pays homage to them and reworks them to new effect. Yu Shu Lien's rooftop pursuit of the mysterious thief recalls similar plot twists in *The Jade Bow*, and her frantic efforts to defeat Jen in the courtyard evoke the climax of *Legendary Weapons of China*, where the old master turns to a panoply of armaments to test his adversary. King Hu would surely have applauded the gentle grace of the floating battle between Jen and Li Mu Bai in the forest, each drifting down to pause effortlessly on gently bobbing branches. Thanks to computer graphics, wires can be erased and figures can be pasted into landscapes with stunning effect—updating the special effects on which the genre has always depended. In the old days the Green Destiny sword's tense quivering would have been rendered in somewhat forced optical effects, but now its tingling energy can be evoked through sound. Indeed, every weapon, every strike and parry, carries a distinct acoustic weight and texture. In reimagining through the most modern means an elemental story of grace and strength, of conflicts between duty and desire, love and the quest for power, *Crouching Tiger, Hidden Dragon* continues a great tradition and brings the *wuxia* triumphantly into the twenty-first century.

—DAVID BORDWELL
Jacques Ledoux Professor of Film Studies at
the University of Wisconsin, Madison;
author of *Planet Hong Kong: Popular
Cinema and the Art of Entertainment*

# CROUCHING TIGER HIDDEN DRAGON

## The Illustrated Screenplay

"FIGHTERS

HAVE

RULES,

TOO:

FRIENDSHIP,

TRUST,

INTEGRITY. . ."

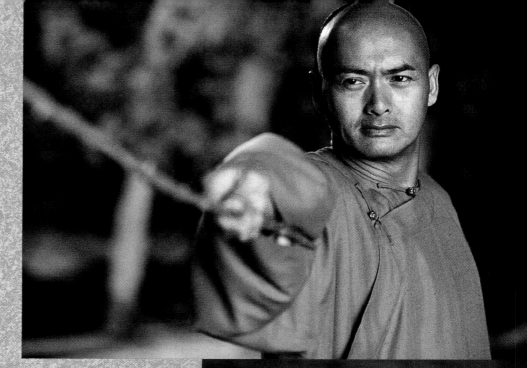

LI MU BAI
CHOW YUN FAT

YU SHU LIEN
MICHELLE YEOH

# Iade Fox
CHENG PEI PEI

## Ien Yu
ZHANG ZIYI

## Lo
CHANG CHEN

Crouching Tiger, Hidden Dragon
*is an epic love story set against
the breathtaking landscapes of
ancient China. The handsome and
powerful Li Mu Bai (Chow Yun Fat),
considered one of the greatest
martial artists of his time, arrives
at the Yuan Security Compound,
run by his longtime friend
(and unspoken love) Yu Shu Lien
(Michelle Yeoh).*

*Li asks Shu Lien, who is on her
way to Beijing, to give his sword
(the legendary Green Destiny)
to Sir Te (Lung Sihung), a respected
leader who was a friend of Shu Lien's
father. Shu Lien is reluctant to take
the sword until Li explains that
he is giving away the Green Destiny
because, after years of fighting, he
wants to follow a new path in life.*

**EXT. YUAN COMPOUND - DAY**
Security men and porters are loading wagons for a convoy. As they work, we see across the lake a lone horseman entering the village. One of the men recognizes him.

> **WORKER**
> Master Li is here!

ANGLE ON: Li Mu Bai, thirties, powerful and handsome.

In the background, old Aunt Wu, at the sight of Li Mu Bai, drops her parcels and runs excitedly into the building.

**INT. YUAN HALLWAY - DAY**
Aunt Wu runs hurriedly through the halls.

> **AUNT WU**
> Shu Lien!

**INT. YU'S ROOM - DAY**
Yu, a beautiful woman in her early 30s, is finishing packing for the convoy, wrapping a few small items in a linen wrapper, as Aunt Wu bursts in.

> **AUNT WU**
> Li Mu Bai is here!

**INT. YUAN PRACTICE HALL - DAY**

> **LI**
> How's everything?

> **AUNT WU**
> Fine. Please come in.

Yu sits, composed, as Aunt Wu ushers Li in. Li carries a large object, wrapped in silk.

Yu smiles.

> **YU**
> Mu Bai . . . It's been too long.

> **LI**
> It has.
> (*he glances around the room*)
> How's business?

> **YU**
> Good. And how are you?

> **LI**
> Fine.

An awkward pause.

> **YU**
> Monk Zheng said you were at Wudan Mountain. He said you were practicing deep meditation.

> **LI**
> Yes.

*Shu Lien tries to persuade Li to join her on her trip to Beijing and present the sword to Sir Te himself. But Li tells her that he is on his way to Wudan Mountain (the training ground for the most skilled warriors) to pay his respects to his late Master, who years ago was poisoned by a notorious female criminal, Jade Fox. He agrees to do his best to meet her later in Beijing.*

**YU**
The mountain must be so peaceful. . . I envy you. My work keeps me so busy, I hardly get any rest.

**LI**
I left the training early.

**YU**
Why? You're a Wudan fighter. Training is everything.

**LI**
During my meditation training. . .
I came to a place of deep silence. . .
I was surrounded by light. . . Time and space disappeared. I had come to a place my master had never told me about.

**YU**
You were enlightened?

**LI**
No. I didn't feel the bliss of enlightenment. Instead. . . I was surrounded by an endless sorrow. I couldn't bear it. I broke off my meditation. I couldn't go on. There was something. . . pulling me back.

**YU**
What was it?

**LI**
Something I can't let go of. You are leaving soon?

**YU**
We're preparing a convoy for a delivery to Peking.

**LI**
Perhaps I could ask you to deliver something to Sir Te for me.

Li unwraps the object. It is an ancient, astonishingly beautiful sword.

**YU**
The Green Destiny Sword? You're giving it to Sir Te?

**LI**
I am. He has always been our greatest protector.

**YU**
I don't understand. How can you part with it? It has always been with you.

**LI**
Too many men have died at its edge. It only looks pure because blood washes so easily from its blade.

**YU**
You use it justly, you're worthy of it.

**LI**
It's time for me to leave it behind.

**YU**
So what will you do now?

Li doesn't reply.

**YU**

Come with me to Peking. You can give the sword to Sir Te yourself. It'll be just like old times.

**LI**

First I must visit my master's grave. It's been many years since Jade Fox murdered him. I have yet to avenge his death. And yet I'm thinking of quitting. I must pray for his forgiveness.

**YU**

Join me once you have finished. I can wait for you in Peking.

**LI**

Perhaps.

**EXT. THE GATE TO PEKING. DAY**
Customs officials have just finished checking the contents in a row of carriages bearing the Sun Security insignia. The caravan slowly passes through the checkpoint into the boundaries of Peking. Yu, riding a handsome horse and clearly the leader, watches as her crew clears inspection.

**GUARDS**

Ok. Pass.

**YU**

Thanks. Let's go into the city.

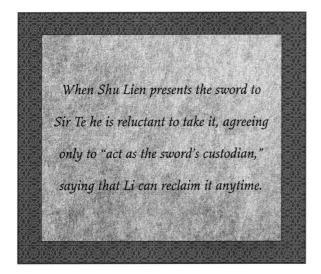

*When Shu Lien presents the sword to Sir Te he is reluctant to take it, agreeing only to "act as the sword's custodian," saying that Li can reclaim it anytime.*

**EXT. OUTSIDE A DEPOT. DAY**
Workers are busy unloading the contents from the carriages. Boss Giao is checking off the merchandise—a cargo of medicinal herbs.

**GIAO**
Everything got here safely. I'm much obliged.

**YU**
Just doing my job.

**GIAO**
Sun Security has been the best since your father started it. You're a credit to his memory.

**YU**
Thank you.

**GIAO**
I mean it.

**EXT. DAY. PEKING**
From a gray tiled roof, we can see Peking's magnificent grid of houses extending miles and miles out, freshly painted by the morning sun.

**EXT. PEKING STREET. DAY**
Dusty and congested as always, people, horses, and carriages are fighting to get through the boulevards.

A group of jugglers perform at a corner.

Yu surveys the busy street from on top of her horse.

**INT. TE'S GREAT HALL - DAY**
Yu presents the sword to Sir Te.

**SIR TE**
This is Li's personal sword, a great hero's weapon! He is the only one in the world worthy of carrying it. It's too fine a gift. I cannot accept it.

**YU**
Sir Te! It has brought him as much trouble as glory. Help him to leave these troubles behind. Otherwise, he'll never be able to start anew.

# ABOUT THE WEAPONRY

The Chinese martial tradition, a bit like Chinese cuisine, presents astonishing variety. The country is so vast, and its local fighting traditions so diverse, that a well-stocked armory indicates a frightening range of ways to inflict damage on other humans.

Central to the *wuxia* mythology is the sword. Chinese distinguish between double-bladed ones, calling them swords proper, and single-bladed ones, which regardless of size and design are usually called knives. There are broadswords like the Green Destiny Sword in *Crouching Tiger, Hidden Dragon* and lighter sabre-like swords, as well as heavy cutlass-like blades (often pierced with rings to snag the opponent's weapon and to distract the opponent with their clanging). Shorter swords are often used in pairs, such as the so-called "butterfly swords," and the *emei*, or blades with arrow-like points at each end.

Western fans often assume that the exotic weaponry on display in *wuxia* films is an invention of moviemakers, but very often it comes from tradition. The simple staff, which may be as long as seven feet, can also have one or two joints (making it useful for delivering a hard, swinging blow or for enclosing an opponent's arm). Bruce Lee popularized the short, jointed staff, best known by its Japanese name, *nunchaku*. Whips may be sectional as well. Spears come in a dazzling variety of shapes, including the jagged-edged "snakehead" spear and the hook-spear. Spears often have colorful tassels or feathers which distract the opponent from the blade's maneuvers. There are hand axes, hammers with heavy spherical heads, and heavy cudgels with bulbous, gourd-shaped heads. For throwing there are darts and arrows, razor-edged stars, and boomerang-style blades, and the infamous "flying guillotine," a rattan basket with an opening lined with knives. During the 1960s and 1970s, many *wuxia pian* built their plots around the sheer variety of Chinese arms. Zhang Che's *New One-Armed Swordsman*, for instance, gave the villain a two-jointed staff, the secondary protagonist a pair of heavy butterfly swords, and the main protagonist a single light broadsword, so the combat was not only among fighters but among weapons and techniques.

—DAVID BORDWELL

*At the home of Sir Te, Shu Lien meets Jen (Zhang Ziyi), the beautiful young daughter of Governer Yu (Li Fa Zeng), a prominent political figure. Jen, seemingly naive and innocent, quickly endears herself to Shu Lien. Jen is apprehensive about her upcoming arranged marriage and speaks longingly of the freedom of being a fighter, probing Shu Lien with questions about the Giang Hu (martial arts life).*

**SIR TE**
All right. I'll act as the sword's custodian.

De Lu, the head servant, enters.

**DE LU**
Governor Yu has arrived.

**SIR TE**
I must change.

**YU**
(*getting up*)
You've always been so good to Li Mu Bai and me. Please accept our thanks.

**SIR TE**
Please do not be such a stranger. You'll stay the night as my guest. Now, Shu Lien. . . tell me something. And forgive me for prying. Your father was a great friend to me, and I think of you as my own daughter.

**YU**
Please, Sir Te, what is it?

**SIR TE**
Li Mu Bai giving up his sword and his warrior days. . . maybe he's trying to tell you something?

**YU**
I don't know. . .

**SIR TE**
Don't be coy. I've always known about your feelings for each other. All these years, it's a shame. . . neither of you is brave enough to admit the truth to the other. You're both wasting precious time.

**YU**
I beg your pardon. Li Mu Bai
and I aren't cowards.

**SIR TE**
When it comes to emotions, even
great heroes can be idiots. Tell me
if Li Mu Bai is not more open the
next time you see him. I'll give
him an earful!

**INT. TE'S STUDY - DAY**
Yu and De Lu approach the study.

**DE LU**
Sir Te said to leave the sword in
here.

De Lu opens the door and is startled
to find a young woman inside. The
woman is studying the sheets of
calligraphy hanging on the walls.

**DE LU**
Who are you?

**JEN**
I'm your guest today. I am
Governor Yu's daughter.

**DE LU**
This is Sir Te's study. You are
here to. . .

**JEN**
I was looking for a quiet corner.

**DE LU**
I am Sir Te's head servant. And this is another of our guests.

**INT. TE'S STUDY - DAY**
Yu gently lays the sword, still in its sheath, in Jen's hands.

>            **JEN**
> It's heavy for such a thin piece
> of metal!

>            **YU**
> The handle is heavy. And the blade
> is no ordinary metal. Still, the
> sword is the lightest of weapons.
> You're just not used to handling it.

>            **JEN**
> But I have had much practice. As a
> child in the West, a platoon lived
> with us. They'd let me play with

## ZHANG ZIYI

their weapons. The scabbard is so beautiful.

>            **YU**
> Beautiful but dangerous. Once
> you see it tainted with blood,
> its beauty is hard to admire.
> It's 400 years old.

>            **JEN**
> Exquisite! You said it belongs to. . .

>            **YU**
> My friend Li Mu Bai. He's given it
> to Sir Te as a gift.

>            **JEN**
> Li Mu Bai! The famous warrior?
> Why would he give his sword
> to Sir Te?

>            **YU**
> You're too young to understand.

>            **JEN**
> You're a sword fighter too?

# FINDING CHINA

Ang Lee came to Bejing, his mother's home, for the first time two years ago, just to see whether he could make a movie there. "I was kind of disappointed," he said. "Other than the palace, everything was modern. I didn't see what I was looking for—it felt as if I were in a big Taipei. I had no thrill because that China does not exist anymore, either in Taiwan or America or here: It's a history. It's a dream that all the Chinese people in the world have, an impression. Gone with the wind.

"But you can't remove China from the boy's head, so I'm finding China now. That's why I'm making this movie with these people, to talk about things we know and that practically don't exist. Good old China."

—JOAN DUPONT

Yu yanks the sword out of the sheath. An eerie sound resonates within the study. Jen is even more impressed.

> **YU**
> Yes, I am. But I prefer the machete. Certain moves, however, call for a sword.

> **JEN**
> Really?

Yu puts the sword back in the case.

> **JEN**
> (*longingly*)
> It must be exciting to be a fighter, to be totally free!

> **YU**
> Fighters have rules too: friendship, trust, integrity . . . Without rules, we wouldn't survive for long.

> **JEN**
> I've read all about people like you. Roaming wild, beating up anyone who gets in your way!

> **YU**
> Writers wouldn't sell many books if they told how it really is.

> **JEN**
> But you're just like the characters in the stories.

**YU**
Sure. No place to bathe for days, sleeping in flea-infested beds. . . They tell you all about that in those books?

**JEN**
You know what I mean. I'm getting married soon, but I haven't lived the life I want.

**YU**
So I heard. Congratulations. It's the most important step in a woman's life, isn't it?

**JEN**
You're not married, are you?

**YU**
What do you think?

**JEN**
No! You couldn't roam around freely if you were.

**YU**
You're probably right.

Yu studies Jen. The room falls silent for a moment.

**EXT. SIDE COURT YARD - DAY**
It's dusk and the sky is a beautiful orange and purple. Jen is leaving the study escorted by her maid. She turns to Yu for a final good-bye. Yu seems intrigued by the encounter.

**EXT. SIR TE'S COMPOUND - NIGHT**
Two lighted lanterns are raised up.

**INT. TE'S STUDY - NIGHT**
Sir Te hands the sword to Governor Yu.

**SIR TE**
Go ahead, Governor Yu.

Governor Yu is impressed by the opulence and elegance of the sword. He closes his eyes to guess the weight of the sword. Te snubs out the flame from a candle, then slides the sword out from its sheath. The sword gives off a luminous blue glow in the dark.

**SIR TE**
Two feet 9 inches long. 1 inch wide. The handle is 1 inch deep, 2.6 inches wide. Seven-tenths of an inch thick. With seven rubies missing from the hilt. You can tell the design dates back to before the Chin era. Engraved with a technique lost by the time of the Han Dynasty.

**GOVERNOR YU**
Your knowledge is remarkable, Sir Te.

**SIR TE**
A sword by itself rules nothing. It

# FIGHTING AS A WAY OF THINKING AND FEELING

**JAMES SCHAMUS:** *Crouching Tiger, Hidden Dragon* is not a kung fu movie that we associate with street fighting. This movie is more about inner strength and centeredness. That's where the floating comes in, more romantic choreography and dance.

**ANG LEE:** I wanted to try something different. Even the movie stars, like Michelle Yeoh, are trained dancers first. And Chow Yun Fat never touched a sword in his life. First and foremost, they are wonderful actors.

I did a lot of vaulting wire work—more than Yuen Wo Ping ever did before. Two of the climactic fights involve two women. He is famous for real macho combat. And the more elaborate camera movement, lighting, beauty, aesthetics. That's not usually what most martial arts films are after.

**JAMES SCHAMUS:** In this film, the acting, the drama has a kind of martial arts choreography to it. It has that kind of grandness and scale. And the martial arts themselves are a kind of dance and very abstract art: motion, editing, movement, image.

**ANG LEE:** Through the martial arts you express how you feel instead of just beating someone up. There is a dramatic quality to it.

**JAMES SCHAMUS:** The people are expressing where they are, their ambiguities and ambivalences, the conflicts they feel. In most of the fights in this movie, the people can't fully fight, because emotionally they are torn. So, the fighting is a way of thinking and feeling and relating.

ABOVE: *Peter Pau, director of photography, and his camera assistant filming a fight scene between Cheng Pei Pei (Jade Fox) and Wang Deming (Tsai).*

comes alive only through skillful manipulation.

**GOVERNOR YU**
I see your point. Please continue.

**SIR TE**
The Imperial Court isn't the problem. With royalty and officials everywhere, the Royal Guard keeps security tight. But Peking is not like the West. Here, you'll find all sorts of characters. Proceed with caution in your quest for law and order. Don't depend only on the court. Contacts in the Giang Hu underworld can ensure your position. Be strong, yet supple. This is the way to rule.

INT. JEN'S ROOM - NIGHT
A maid warms her hands in a basin of hot water for Jen, then walks over to Jen and helps remove her earrings. Someone knocks and the maid goes to answer the door.

**MAID**
Governess. . .

**GOVERNESS**
Let me do it.

The maid leaves as the governess enters the room.

**JEN**
Please sit.

**GOVERNESS**
I've made you silk pajamas. Do you want to change into them?

**JEN**
Put them down.

**GOVERNESS**
I heard you met Shu Lien today.

**JEN**
Do you know her?

**GOVERNESS**
She's one of those. Your mother would not want you consorting with her kind.

Jen shoots her an angry look.

**JEN**
I'll socialize with whomever I please.

**GOVERNESS**
Don't invite danger into your father's house.

She's about to say something, then thinks better of it.

**JEN**
I'm tired now.

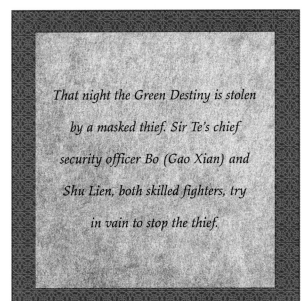

*That night the Green Destiny is stolen by a masked thief. Sir Te's chief security officer Bo (Gao Xian) and Shu Lien, both skilled fighters, try in vain to stop the thief.*

**GOVERNESS**
Go to bed then. Miss has grown up, and is getting married soon. God knows what the future will bring.

**JEN**
It will be just the same. Enough! I'm tired.

**GOVERNESS**
Autumn is coming. I'll shut the windows for you.

The governess leaves. Jen sits on the side of her bed, thinking.

**EXT. TE'S COMPOUND - NIGHT**
A wide shot of the compound. A patrol man greets Master Bo, Sir Te's head of security. The place is serene.

**MASTER BO**
Chilly, eh?

**NIGHTMAN**
Yes, Master Bo.

As Bo walks on, shadows rustle in a treetop in the background.

**EXT./INT. INSIDE AND OUTSIDE OF TE'S STUDY - NIGHT**
A masked figure silently opens the window and enters the room. It moves swiftly to the sword case, opens it, and wraps the sword.

Bo enters, sees the thief, who leaps up to the ceiling. The thief steps over Bo and out into the courtyard. Bo tries to stop the thief, who easily outwits him, jumping onto the roof as Bo yells out.

**BO**
Someone help! Stop him! He's on the roof! The sword's been stolen! Stop thief! Stop him!

The thief skips a few times and jumps off to a side street.

## LOCATION: SHOOTING IN CHINA

This film was shot in almost every corner of China, including the Gobi Desert and the Taklamakan Plateau, north of Tibet, near the Kyrgyzstan border. We were based for a time in Urumchi, where all the street signs are in Chinese and Arabic. Then all the way down south to the Bamboo Forest in Anji and north to Cheng De, where the famous summer palace is. The studio work was done in Beijing; we recorded the music in Shanghai. The background vocals for the end credit song were recorded in Los Angeles and we did post-production looping in Hong Kong. So it is really bringing together almost every conceivable idea you could have of China.

—JAMES SCHAMUS

Bo grabs a pole and runs, as gongs begin to sound, alerting people to the theft. People rush outside, Yu Shu Lien among them.

**EXT. PEKING STREET - NIGHT**
Bo runs through the streets. The thief is nowhere in sight. Suddenly, there are sounds of weapons clashing. Bo hurries towards the source.

**EXT. AN ALLEY OUTSIDE GOVERNOR YU'S COMPOUND - NIGHT**
Bo is surprised to see the hooded figure battling with two other fighters—Tsai (male, 40s) and May, his daughter.

**TSAI**
It's Jade Fox!

**MAY**
We must avenge mother!

The hooded figure does a gravity defying flip and soars over a wall, just as Bo arrives.

**BO**
Do something! He's getting away!

**EXT. PEKING ROOFTOP - NIGHT**
The thief runs atop a roof—right into Yu. Yu and the hooded figure face off.

> **YU**
> Return the sword, and I'll let you go.

The figure just regards her, slightly shifting weight.

Yu attacks, but the figure repels her.

> **YU**
> You've been trained at Wudan?

The figure answers by leaping to another rooftop. Yu catches up, and resumes her attack with a relentless series of lightning-quick blows.

**EXT. ALLEY OUTSIDE GOVERNOR YU'S COMPOUND - NIGHT**
Bo follows Tsai and May, who are quickly walking away.

> **TSAI**
> You're mistaken. We're just street performers. We were rehearsing.

> **MAY**
> Father!

> **BO**
> You were rehearsing? Who are you trying to fool?

May wants to respond but is again cut off by Tsai. They run off.

## SETS AND COSTUMES

In *Crouching Tiger, Hidden Dragon*, we focused on size, space, lighting, fabric texture, and blocks of color to accentuate character movement. Most importantly, we wanted to break from the tradition of martial arts films. We eliminated a lot of details from the real environment and attempted a few daring experiments. We wanted to create a large space within the film. To accentuate the character's motion, we pushed back all the unnecessary props and structures, creating a large area in the foreground. Many hidden symbols appear within the same space. We toned down colors to establish a sense of void, so subtle changes of color and texture would become more obvious. For example, Chow Yun Fat's four robes are the same style but made with different fabrics. Also, Jen's embroidered landscape robe, the transparent landscapes in Te's library, and Jen's room were all meant to express shadows of two co-existing worlds.

—Tim Yip, Production and Costume Designer

The news of the theft of the Green Destiny quickly spreads throughout the city and, as the investigation gets under way, suspicion is cast in many directions. Bo announces that he tracked the thief back to Governor Yu's compound. Police Inspector Tsai (Wang De Ming) and his daughter May (Li Li), a team of skilled martial artists from the countryside, claim that the thief is none other than Jade Fox, who also killed Tsai's wife. But Shu Lien has her own suspicions, which she is reluctant to share with the others until she can investigate further.

# WIRE WORK

*Crouching Tiger*'s most eye-catching sequences (including Lee's favorite, an electrifying battle along the tops of tall bamboo) are the flying-over-the-rooftops and climbing-up-walls stunts that are most characteristic of the genre. The technique is called wire work because it involves suspending the actors high in the air off of cables, a tricky and dangerous business. "Each actor can take from 5 up to 20 people to manipulate. There's a lot of calculation and coordination involved," Ang Lee says. "When the shot is over, the guys fall on the ground, they are so tired. Sometimes they start to barf."

Lee, however, was not going to be satisfied with just action. Traditionally, the Hong Kong–based genre is short on characterization and emotional nuance. Lee soon found out why "it's almost against nature" to do the kind of film he envisioned.

"Shooting the action is traditionally a very time-consuming process, with lots and lots of shots and time to set up," he explains. "On a 100-day shooting schedule, maybe 80 days would be spent on the martial arts scenes, 20 days to do the rest, so they don't have time to get into the script."

More than that, "demands for dramatic reality and performance could be distracting for the actors. In martial-arts films, you have to focus on hitting the right beat so you don't poke the other person in the eye. If you're thinking about doing something genuine at the same time, it could be dangerous."

—Kenneth Turan

ABOVE: *In the first chase scene, Michelle Yeoh pursues the masked thief of the Green Destiny. This behind-the-scene photograph shows the wires that secured the actors and the position of the roving camera.*

BO

Where did that thief go?

Bo looks around and discovers he had chased the thief into Governor Yu's compound.

BO

Governor Yu's house!

**EXT. ROOF TOP**
Yu and the Black Figure continue to fight.

YU

Get down here! Give back the sword!

**EXT. GOVERNOR YU'S - NIGHT**
Yu slowly gets the upper hand in her fight with the thief. A small arrow cuts across the night and flies toward Yu. She catches it, but the masked figure takes the opportunity to get away.

Yu pauses to feel the arrow in her hand, standing in the empty courtyard.

**EXT. TE'S SIDE ENTRANCE - DAY**
De Lu escorts Yu into Te's.

DE LU

Sir Te awaits you.

**INT. TE'S GREAT HALL - DAY**
Men are standing at attention. Bo is giving his account of what happened, as Yu enters.

BO

I'm sure the thief is in the Yu household.

SIR TE

How dare you imply?

BO

But I saw—

SIR TE

—Enough.

The men hustle out. Bo can barely contain his frustration.

YU

Has Governor Yu ever seen the sword?

SIR TE

Yes, though I doubt he's involved in this.

YU

But the sword could be in his compound.

SIR TE

Then someone's trying to set him up. We should inform Li Mu Bai.

*Shu Lien goes to Governor Yu's compound to visit Jen. Jen, who is still apprehensive about her impending marriage, tells Shu Lien that she wishes she could live the Giang Hu life and enjoy the freedom of Shu Lien and Li Mu Bai. Shu Lien tries to quell Jen's schoolgirl fantasies by telling her the reality of her relationship with Li—Shu Lien was once engaged to another man, who was a brother by oath to Li Mu Bai. After her fiancé was killed defending Li in battle, Li and Shu Lien grew closer and wanted to be together, but they could not dishonor her fiancé's memory. Shu Lien explains that, even though she lives the Giang Hu life, as a woman she still has to abide by tradition. As Shu Lien leaves the Yu compound, she is watched by Jen's sinister governess.*

## EXT. OUTSIDE GOVERNOR YU'S COMPOUND - NIGHT

Madam Yu is returning from temple. The governess is helping her out of the carriage. Servants are peeling bills off a wall across the street.

### MADAM YU
What is it?

### MAID
Madam Yu, someone's put up posters.

A partially torn flyer with the words "Jade Fox will not escape justice!" is seen on the ground.

### MADAM YU
Let me see.

### GOVERNESS
Someone is after Jade Fox. Preposterous, looking for her here!

Madam Yu nods and walks inside, as the Governess tosses the flyer away and follows her. A hand scoops up the flyer —it is Yu. She studies it, then puts it in her pocket, and moves on.

## EXT. BRIDGE - DAY

Bo is searching for the Tsais. The bridge is full of jugglers. But the two are nowhere to be found.

**EXT. PEKING STREET - DAY**
Bo quizzes a homeless man.

**BO**

Where are they?

**HOMELESS MAN**

I don't know. I haven't seen them in two days.

Bo is about to give up when he looks up and sees May walking quickly into an alley. Bo follows her.

**EXT. IN FRONT OF TSAI'S HOUSE**
May walks into a dilapidated house surrounded by a broken-down bamboo fence. Bo inches closer and sees May and Tsai oiling their weapons.

**INT. BO'S ROOM - DAY**
Jen practices calligraphy. The governess is by her side embroidering and throwing occasional glances at Jen. The maid enters.

**MAID**

There is a Miss Shu Lien here to see you.

Jen stops and looks up at them.

**GOVERNESS**

Miss is busy right now.

**MAID**

I'll tell her.

**JEN**

Show her in.

The governess shoots her a look.

**GOVERNESS**
This spells trouble.

**JEN**
I have a guest.

The governess gets up to leave just as the maid shows Yu in.

**MAID**
This way please.

The governess and Yu exchange quick glances. The governess bows slightly and departs.

**JEN**
I've missed you.

**YU**
How so?

**JEN**
I'm bored.

Yu sees the calligraphy.

**YU**
You're doing calligraphy?

**JEN**
I'll write your name. Just for fun.

Jen writes Yu's name with great confidence and swiftness.

**YU**
I never realized my name looks like "sword."

Jen freezes slightly.

**YU**
You write gracefully. Calligraphy is so similar to fencing.

**JEN**
Maybe it is. I wouldn't know.

The maid enters with tea.

**JEN**
Please.

**YU**
Thank you for seeing me. I hear your wedding day is near. You must be overwhelmed by the preparations.

**JEN**
I'm hardly doing a thing. The less I think of it the better. My parents are arranging everything. The Gous are a very powerful family. My marrying one will be good for my father's career.

**YU**
You are fortunate to marry into such a noble family.

**JEN**

Am I? I wish I were like the heroes in the books I read. Like you and Li Mu Bai. I guess I'm happy to be marrying. But to be free to live my own life, to choose whom I love. . . That is true happiness.

**YU**

Do you think so? Let me tell you a story.

**JEN**

About you and Li Mu Bai?

**YU**

Yes. Did you know I was once engaged to be married?

**JEN**

No, really?

**YU**

His name was Meng Si Zhao. He was a brother to Li Mu Bai by oath. One day, while in battle, he was killed by the sword of Li Mu Bai's enemy. After, Li Mu Bai and I went through a lot together. Our feelings for each other grew stronger. But how could we dishonor Meng's memory? So the freedom you talk about, I too desire it. But I have never tasted it.

## MICHELLE YEOH ON SPEAKING MANDARIN

I spent so much time practicing Mandarin. I don't think I studied this hard at school, even for exams. I was at such a disadvantage—I don't even read Chinese. So I had a dialogue coach with me every day for three hours. Fortunately Ang had the script down pretty much, so I would say to him, "You're not allowed to change anything. I need at least three days before that scene." I spent a lot of the time remembering the different sounds. It's like learning Shakespeare; every single word needs the right intonation. I had to say all these things that I had never heard of in my entire life, so I spent a lot of time just memorizing, in the car, talking during meals, and so on.

**JEN**

Too bad for Meng, but it's not your fault, or Li Mu Bai's.

**YU**

I am not an aristocrat, as you are. . . but I must still respect a woman's duties.

**JEN**

Don't distance us. From now on, let's be like sisters.

**YU**

Then as a sister, let me wish you happiness in your marriage.

**EXT. YU'S GARDEN - DAY**

The maid escorts Yu out. Yu pauses, looks around, and sees the profile of the Governess peering at her from around a corner.

**INT. JEN'S ROOM - NIGHT**

Moonlight spills into the room, as Jen rises sleeplessly from bed and looks out the window. A light breeze stirs her hair. The sound of the wind rises, and slowly her face dissolves, into. . .

**I/E. CARRIAGE/MONGOLIAN DESERT - DAY**

. . . the face of a younger, less sophisticated Jen, as she lets the dry desert air flow through her hair. She sits in a carriage, part of a caravan, with guards on horseback, that is traveling through the spectacular desert. Across from her sits her mother, of whom she is barely cognizant.

**MADAM YU**

What a godforsaken place! Can't your father be appointed closer to civilization? Jen. . . are you listening to me?

Jen is still looking out the side of the carriage, at a beautiful mountainside.

**INT. JEN'S ROOM - NIGHT**

Jen sighs, and turns back toward her bed.

**EXT. STREET OUTSIDE GOVERNOR YU'S COMPOUND - NIGHT**

Tsai and May have been sitting, hidden in the branches of a tree, watching Jen.

**TSAI**

Let's go!

They drop down silently and walk away. From another rooftop, Lo looks silently on.

**EXT. TSAI'S HOUSE - NIGHT**

Tsai and May enter the house.

**INT. TSAI'S HOUSE - NIGHT**

Inside the tiny house, they discover a hooded figure going through their belongings.

Immediately Tsai throws a knife, which rips off the figure's mask—revealing Bo. Tsai has another long knife at his throat.

TSAI
Who are you?

BO
Wait! I'm a friend!

Tsai pauses.

**INT. TSAI'S HOUSE ~ NIGHT (LATER)**
May fans a small coal-fired grill that is boiling a sizzling pot of vegetable and meatball soup. Her father and Bo are now friendly dinner companions, much to May's delight.

TSAI
I don't care about your sword.

BO
Why were you spying on the Yus?

TSAI
I'm looking for someone. Jade Fox. I'm a police inspector from Shaan Xi, Gen Su district. Jade Fox is a master criminal. I hear she infiltrated the Yus. She must have come with them when they transferred here. But with Yu's reputation, I can't just go in and accuse her.

BO
This Jade Fox is a woman?

TSAI
Yes.

BO
Then leave her to me.

**TSAI**
Pardon me, but I doubt you can
handle her. My wife was quite a
martial arts expert. Jade Fox killed
her. So you see, this is personal.
Leave her to me.

**MAY**
It's ready! (*re: the soup*)

**BO**
I'm ready for anything!

Bo fishes into the pot with his
chopsticks. May intercepts him with
her own chopsticks.

**MAY**
Father gets first dip.

Tsai stiffens and snaps his chopsticks,
not to pick up a meatball but to catch
an incoming dart. A dart wrapped
with a note. Bo jumps up.

**TSAI**
They're gone.

**MAY**
What does it say?

**TSAI**
"We'll settle this at midnight
on Yellow Hill." Good, the fox
is out of her hole.

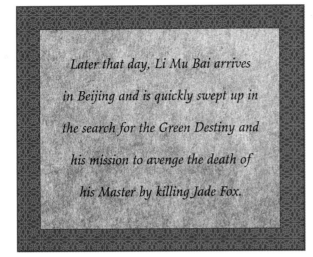

*Later that day, Li Mu Bai arrives in Beijing and is quickly swept up in the search for the Green Destiny and his mission to avenge the death of his Master by killing Jade Fox.*

**INT. TE'S STUDY - NIGHT**
Yu is ushered into the room, to discover Sir Te talking to another man, whose back is to her.

> **SIR TE**
> Shu Lien, look who's here.

The man turns around—it's Li Mu Bai.

**EXT. TE'S HALL - NIGHT**
Yu and Li Mu Bai sit together.

> **LI**
> Sir Te believes it's a ploy to cast suspicion on Governor Yu.

> **YU**
> But something is going on at the Yu household.

> **LI**
> What have you discovered?

From her sleeve, Yu removes the flyer. Li takes it, his face darkening.

> **LI**
> Jade Fox? Impossible.

> **YU**
> You always suspected she'd fled to the West.

> **LI**
> I didn't think she'd dare come back to Peking!

# So I shall Avenge my master's death after all,

**YU**
Is there any place safer than under the nose of Governor Yu?

**LI**
So I shall avenge my master's death after all.

**YU**
Be careful. Sir Te requires discretion. Official business is difficult enough. Don't let personal feelings make it worse. And I don't know. . . even this poster. . . could be some sort of trap.

## ON LANGUAGE

I write in English, it's rewritten into Mandarin, then I have it translated back into English. Going from English to Mandarin, and back into English is like crossing five oceans—by sail. You are going to another mental place. For the subtitles, we go to the original English text, move through the Chinese, and come back to English subtitles. I adapted a particular style to write this screenplay: the "international subtitle" style.

—JAMES SCHAMUS

# WORKING WITH CHOW YUN FAT

**JAMES SCHAMUS:** When Chow flew into Beijing, they literally shut down customs at the airport for forty-five minutes—

**ANG LEE:** While all the customs officers lined up for an autograph.

**JAMES SCHAMUS:** That's the level of stardom that he has.

**ANG LEE:** On set he is like Mr. Perfect. He is very noble. He knows the crew members' names.

**JAMES SCHAMUS:** His wife would leave the set for a moment, and two minutes later he would be suspended, suspended 70 feet on a wire. "Where is my husband? Oh, my God, what are you doing up there?"

**ANG LEE:** Upside down.

**JAMES SCHAMUS:** He would do anything for the film.

**MICHELLE YEOH:** I've waited 15 years to work with this guy. Ang Lee called us over after the first shot we did together and said, "Look at you two." There was chemistry and the scenes were really, really intense. The film has many elements but none overpower the others. Usually in martial arts films the action is the focus, but in this movie there is such a balance. It's emotional, it's dramatic, it transcends everything.

**PETER PAU** (Director of Photography): Chow Yun Fat's first shot was on wires, flying down from a twenty-foot tree. He did eighteen takes. The graveyard fight took fifteen nights of main and second unit photography to complete, double the length we estimated. I worked with Chow on three previous films (*The Greatest Lover, The Killer,* and *Shaolin Jet*). He is kind, sincere, and humorous at all times, definitely one of the most enjoyable actors in the business.

ABOVE: *Chow Yun Fat, Ang Lee, and Sylvia Liu, First Assistant Director.*

**LI**
Did you see who posted it?

Yu pauses.

**YU**
No.

**LI**
It says Jade Fox is hiding at Yu's. On the night of the theft there was a brawl near Yu's. Were you involved?

**YU**
It was Bo, Sir Te's man. I hear he followed the thief to the Yus'.

**LI**
Have you questioned him yet?

**YU**
No, not yet. . .

**LI**
But your men are watching over Yu's compound?

**YU**
No, I'd already sent them home. You can blame me for losing the sword, but please trust that I'll get it back soon using my own methods.

**LI**
That's not what I meant. I don't care about the sword.

**YU**
What do you mean? Didn't you come back here for it?

**LI**
I didn't know it was stolen until I got here.

**YU**
Then, why did you come?

**LI**
Well, we had talked. . .

De Lu enters.

**DE LU**
Pardon my intrusion. Master Li, your room is ready.

**LI**
Thank you. Please lead the way.

**EXT. YELLOW HILL - NIGHT**
Tsai, Bo, and May wait under an ancient tree. Bo stifles a yawn.

**BO**
The fox doesn't care much for punctuality. Still no sign of her.

An old lady struggles up the hill, wearing a floppy hat over her face, holding a cane. The three exchange glances.

*Jade Fox (Cheng Pei Pei) arranges a meeting with Tsai and May to settle their feud once and for all. Security officer Bo, who has developed a fondness for May, insists on accompanying them. At their meeting, Jade Fox reveals her true identity: Since her murder of Li's Master, she has taken cover as Jen Yu's governess.*

*A fierce battle ensues between Jade Fox and her adversaries. Tsai, May, and Bo fight skillfully but are only able to keep her at bay until Li Mu Bai arrives. Li is about to defeat Jade Fox when the masked thief appears to assist her, with the Green Destiny in hand. Jade Fox kills Tsai and escapes with her masked accomplice.*

**TSAI**
Enough! Show yourself.

The old woman shrinks in fear, but then throws off her disguise and unveils herself—the Governess.

**FOX**
Tsai. . . you dog! You will pay for your stubbornness.

**BO**
That's what you think, old witch!

**TSAI**
If you surrender now, you'll suffer less. But if you resist, I won't stop until you're dead.

**MAY**
Father! Let me avenge my mother's death.

**FOX**
You'll soon end up like her, you little whore!

**BO**
You'll pay for that!

A fierce battle begins, the main fighting between Tsai and Fox, with May and Bo getting a stab in occasionally, when the opportunity presents itself.

**TSAI** (*to Bo*)
She's going to paralyze you!

Using acupressure, Fox disables Bo. May shoots an arrow at her, but she catches it and flings it back, hitting May.

**TSAI**
May!

Fox then disables Tsai, but just as she goes for the kill, Li Mu Bai flies down from the treetops and steps between them.

**FOX**
Tsai, you filthy mongrel! An ambush!

**MAY**
Father, are you all right?

Li addresses Fox.

**LI**
Wudan should have gotten rid of you long ago. It's been a long time, Jade Fox! You don't remember me. . . But you should remember my master. You infiltrated Wudan while I was away. You stole our secret manual and poisoned our master! Now it's time for you to pay!

**FOX**
Your master underestimated us women. Sure, he'd sleep with me, but he would never teach me. He deserved to die by a woman's hand!

FATHER? LET ME AVENGE MY MOTHER'S DEATH.

**LI**
You stole the secrets of Wudan's highest martial arts. But after ten years of training, your moves are still undisciplined. And today, under a Wudan sword. . . you will die!

Li easily brings Fox to the ground.

Li raises his sword to the prostrate Fox. A figure masked in black appears next to Fox, sword extended, saving her.

**FOX**
Disciple, we'll kill them all!

**FIGURE IN BLACK**
Let's go!

**BO**
Another one!

**FOX**
I must get rid of Tsai!

Fox fights Tsai, Bo, and May, as Li addresses the masked figure.

**LI**
Who are you? Why is the Green Destiny in your possession?

**FIGURE IN BLACK**
What's it to you?

**LI**
My name is Li Mu Bai. The Green Destiny is mine. Jade Fox can't be your master. Where did you learn that "Xuan Piu" move?

**FIGURE IN BLACK**
I'm just playing around.

## ON FLYING

People fly in this movie but I ask for real emotion from them. I may have underestimated the power of gravity; it's tough on actors. Usually an actor doesn't do that many stunts, and the stuntman doesn't do that much acting; in this movie, they have to do both.

—ANG LEE

**LI**
Tell me, who is your master?

**FIGURE IN BLACK**
Let's go!

**FOX**
We must kill them!

Tsai throws his blade at Fox, who catches it and throws it back, hitting him in the head. Fox and the masked figure leap away.

May drops to the ground, cradling her dead father's head. Bo kneels beside her.

**MAY**
Father!

*The following day, Shu Lien asks Sir Te to invite Jen Yu and her mother to his home for tea, so she can investigate her suspicions about the identity of the masked thief. Shu Lien tells Jen and Madam Yu (Hai Yan) of Jade Fox's villainous acts, and hints that if the Green Destiny is returned the thief will not be persecuted, all the time watching Jen's reactions.*

**EXT. TE'S - DAY**
Te and a group of his men look down as a cloth is removed from over the body of Tsai. Bo and May stand before them.

**TE**
This is Tsai?

**MAY**
My father. Police Inspector from Shaan.

**TE**
This should be reported to Governor Yu. The victim is an officer. You believe the killer is hiding out in his compound?

**YU**
I'd bet my life on it!

**TE** (*to Li and Yu*)
Come with me.

He exits the room.

**INT. TE'S STUDY - DAY**
Te, Li, and Yu are seated.

**SIR TE**
This needs to be resolved, and quickly.

**LI**
I'll get into the Yu household and get her. I'll ferret out Fox and her gang.

**YU**
We must be careful. Governor Yu is a court official, and in charge of security. Any disturbance will cast suspicion on him. It might get Sir Te in trouble.

**SIR TE**
This is a delicate matter.

**YU**
Sir Te, can you find some excuse
to invite Madam Yu and her
daughter?

**SIR TE**
What do you have in mind?

**YU**
The best way to trap a fox is
through her cubs.

Sir Te and Li look puzzled.

**EXT. SIR TE'S GARDEN - DAY**
Yu sits with Madam Yu and Jen. They
busy themselves with various items
for her trousseau.

**MADAM YU**
Madam Te is certainly spoiling us
with these wedding gifts. She's
being so considerate.

**YU**
I'm sorry she's not feeling well
enough to receive you today.

**MADAM YU**
I heard Sir Te lost something.
And now Madame Te's not
feeling well. . .

Jen sits silently reading.

**YU**
We know who stole the missing

item. If the thief returns it, I'm sure Sir Te will pursue the matter no further.

**MADAM YU**

That's good. Sometimes the help can't keep their hands to themselves. It's very embarrassing.

**YU**

Sir Te knows that even well-meaning people can make mistakes. . . that can bring ruin to themselves and their families.

**MADAM YU**

But don't be too lenient.

## WANG DU LU

Wang Du Lu, the author of the original novel upon which *Crouching Tiger* was based, was born to a poor family in Beijing in 1909. He suffered from poverty and illness in his early childhood, which prevented him from receiving a formal education. Wang started writing when he was twenty, mainly social realist drama and martial arts novels, both of which manifested a strong sense of pathos and tragic sentiment in his characters. He was appointed as the People's Representative of Shenyang in 1956. With the outbreak of the Cultural Revolution in the 1960s, martial arts novels were banned and writers of the genre were prosecuted.

Wang died of Parkinson's disease in 1977.

# WHAT THE TITLE MEANS

*Crouching Tiger, Hidden Dragon:* For those familiar with the Chinese characters, the link between the film's title and the story line is graphically clear—Jen has the word for "dragon" embedded in her name, while Lo, her lover, is the tiger. Jen and Lo are headstrong, self-centered, and wild—and young. In contrast, Li Mu Bai and Shu Lien respect the ideals of honor and selfless duty—acting as role models within the story, and to the larger audience.

The film is in two parts. Today, "Crouching Tiger, Hidden Dragon" is a common expression, which reminds us never to underestimate the mysteries, the potent characters that lie beneath the surface of society. But for me, the true meaning of the film lies with the "Hidden Dragon." *Crouching Tiger, Hidden Dragon* is a story about passions, emotions, desires—the dragons hidden inside all of us.

So as Li Mu Bai and Shu Lien pursue Jen, they are chasing their own dragons. Jen's youth and energy remind them of the romance and freedom that neither of them has experienced. Having chosen a life of duty, Li Mu Bai and Shu Lien had to suppress their passions and desires, and, most of all, their love for each other. It is always close to the surface, but if they gave in to their true feelings, they would be abandoning the code of honor that shaped their lives.

—ANG LEE

**YU**

No mercy will be shown toward the murderer who turned up in Peking.

**MADAME YU**

A murderer?

**YU**

Yes. The very killer of Li Mu Bai's own master. Last night, she killed a policeman who had tracked her down.

**MADAME YU**

A female criminal! Now that's news!

Jen becomes visibly upset.

**JEN**

You say she killed a policeman?

**YU**

Yes, from the West. He went undercover and followed her here.

**MADAM YU**

Maybe the murderer and the thief are one and the same.

**YU**

I doubt it. This thief. . . is very unusual. . .

As Yu speaks, she lifts the tea pot to

*That night, the masked thief creeps into Te's study to return the Green Destiny, but is intercepted by Li Mu Bai. They begin to fight. The masked thief is skilled but doesn't have the training of Li Mu Bai. He offers to take the thief to Wudan Mountain to train as his protégé. The thief begins to imitate Li's graceful style but rebuffs his offer.*

pour Jen some tea. As she finishes speaking, she looks into Jen's face and the pot slips from her hand. Without even looking down, Jen instinctively catches the pot with a lightning-fast move.

> **YU**
> . . . And most likely smarter than a mere killer.

Sir Te and Li Mu Bai walk by.

> **JEN**
> (*formal*)
> Greetings, Sir Te.

> **SIR TE**
> Hello, Madam Yu. This is Li Mu Bai, the renowned swordsman.

> **LI**
> Delighted to meet you.

Li sizes Jen up.

> **TE**
> Miss Yu is soon to be married.

> **LI**
> Congratulations.

**EXT. TSAI'S HOUSE - NIGHT**
May opens her door, only to find Bo standing guard.

> **MAY**
> Why don't you come in?

> **BO**
> I'm standing guard.

> **MAY**
> Come in. It's cold.

She turns back inside, hesitates, then turns back to him.

**MAY**
Come in. We don't have to fear
Jade Fox if we're together.

**EXT. TE COMPOUND - NIGHT**
A still, dark night.

**EXT. TE'S STUDY - NIGHT**
Something moves in the moonlight. A
hooded figure jumps down.

Li Mu Bai, who had been hiding in the
shadows, comes forward.

**LI**
Isn't it a bit too late to be out?
You've brought me the sword?

**FIGURE**
I do as I please.

The masked figure lunges away, but Li
Mu Bai leaps with incredible speed and
grabs the sword from her.

**LI**
Where's your master?

**FIGURE**
What's it to you?

The figure floats away. Li chases
after her.

**EXT. PEKING STREET - NIGHT**
The two fly over houses and bounce off
of rooftops, displaying amazing
floating skills.

**INT. ABANDONED MONASTERY -
NIGHT**
The figure bounces into an old
monastery. Li is already there.

**LI**
Had enough flying?  You've got
potential. You've studied the Wudan
Manual but you don't understand it.
You need a real master.

The figure doesn't respond, but we
sense the pride in her eyes.

**FIGURE**
Do you think you are a real
master?

**LI**
Like most things, I am nothing.
It's the same for this sword. All
of it is simply a state of mind.

**FIGURE**
Stop talking like a monk!
Just fight!

**LI**
Then tell me where Jade Fox is.

**FIGURE**
On guard!

# No growth without assistance, No action without reaction, No desire without restraint,

LI
Real sharpness comes without effort.

**EXT. MONASTERY - NIGHT**
The figure leaps into the garden, but again, Li is ahead of her.

The figure attacks Li, who uses his agility to evade her. Frustrated, the figure intensifies her attack.

The figure, losing composure, attacks wildly. Li gets even more elusive, using a branch to repel her.

LI
No growth without assistance. No action without reaction. No desire without restraint. Now give yourself up and find yourself again. There is a lesson for you.

Li now holds the stick to her mask, gently raising it slightly.

FIGURE
Go ahead.

LI
Why should I? You need practice. I can teach you to fight with the Green Destiny, but first you must learn to hold it in stillness.

80

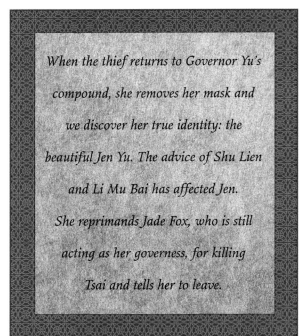

*When the thief returns to Governor Yu's compound, she removes her mask and we discover her true identity: the beautiful Jen Yu. The advice of Shu Lien and Li Mu Bai has affected Jen. She reprimands Jade Fox, who is still acting as her governess, for killing Tsai and tells her to leave.*

The figure's eyes cloud with tears.

FIGURE
Wudan is a whorehouse! Keep your lessons!

The figure swirls and takes off, leaving a rueful Li standing alone in the monastery.

**INT. JEN'S ROOM - NIGHT**
Jen slips in through the window. She pulls off her mask, as she spots the Governess/Fox sitting and sewing.

FOX
You're home late. . . or should I say early?

JEN
Why are you still here? You killed a policeman. You should leave! You'll bring ruin on my whole family.

FOX
They wouldn't have found me if you hadn't stolen the sword. Like a little girl, you thought stealing would be fun? You, too, are responsible for that death. Come with me. You don't want to waste your life as the wife of some bureaucrat. Denied your talent. . . As a master and disciple we will rule.

FIGURE
Why do you want to teach me?

LI
I've always wanted a disciple worthy of Wudan's secrets.

FIGURE
And if I use them to kill you?

LI
That's a risk I'm willing to take. Deep down, you're good. Even Jade Fox couldn't corrupt you.

**JEN**

I'll never live as a thief!

**FOX**

You're already a thief.

**JEN**

That was just for fun. How can I leave? Where would I go?

**FOX**

Wherever we want. We'll get rid of anyone in our way. Even your father.

**JEN**

Shut up!

**FOX**

It's the Giang Hu fighter lifestyle. . . kill or be killed. Exciting, isn't it?

**JEN**

I owe you nothing.

**FOX**

Yes, you do! You are still my disciple.

Jen lunges at the Governess, and the two exchange a few blows. Jen presses her finger against one of the Governess's pressure points, disabling her. Jen pushes her across the room.

**JEN**

You think you've been teaching me

# SENSE AND SENSIBILITY

In discussing *Crouching Tiger*, Mr. Lee frequently made comparisons to *Sense and Sensibility*, his acclaimed 1995 adaptation of Jane Austen's novel, written by and starring Emma Thompson. It was the witty, subtle, Austen-like perception of social bonds and tensions, apparent in his Chinese-language family dramas, *The Wedding Banquet* and *Eat Drink Man Woman*, that led Ms. Thompson to ask Mr. Lee to direct his first major English-language film.

"Family dramas and *Sense and Sensibility* are all about conflict, about family obligations versus free will," he said. The martial arts form "externalizes the elements of restraint and exhilaration," he continued, punching his fist outward. "In a family drama there is a verbal fight. Here you kick butt."

—ERICK ECKHOLM

## THE MUSIC

The music in this film draws from grand Chinese traditions and also from Western orchestral music, and ethnic and pop music, and really pulls all of them together. It was written by Tan Dun, who composed the most recent Peter Sellars opera, *Peony Pavillion*, and was the musical director last year at Tanglewood. He works in both China and the U.S. And the great Yo-Yo Ma plays the cello solos.

—JAMES SCHAMUS

all these years from the manual? You couldn't even decipher the symbols!

**FOX**
I studied the diagrams. But you hid the details!

**JEN**
You wouldn't have understood, even if I had tried to explain. You know. . . you've gone as far as you can go. I hid my skills so as not to hurt you.

**FOX**
If I hadn't seen you fight with Li Mu Bai, I'd still be ignorant of all you've hidden from me.

**JEN**
Master. . . I started learning from you in secret when I was 10. You enchanted me with the world of Giang Hu. But once I realized I could surpass you, I became so frightened! Everything fell apart. I had no one to guide me, no one to learn from.

**FOX**
Believe me, I've a lesson or two left to teach you!

Fox exits.

**EXT. GOVERNOR YU'S GATE ~ DAY**
The Governess leaves, a small sack over her back.

**EXT. TE'S COURTYARD ~ DAY**
Li practices fluently with Green Destiny in hand, beautifully at ease with the weapon. He spins around to find Yu standing in the doorway.

**YU**
The sword is back. . . are you happy?

Li smiles.

**LI**

I admit, getting it back makes me realize how much I'd missed it.

**YU**

But it's not your sword anymore. You gave it to Sir Te.

**LI**

True. But I must borrow it for one last mission. Jade Fox must die at its edge. Did you know what you were hiding when you covered for that girl?

**YU**

My job was to get the sword back, without embarrassing anyone. I wasn't about to ruin her life, or her father's.

THE SWORD

IS BACK, , ,

ARE YOU

HAPPY?

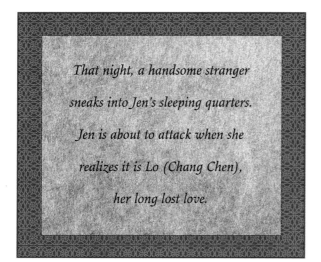

*That night, a handsome stranger sneaks into Jen's sleeping quarters. Jen is about to attack when she realizes it is Lo (Chang Chen), her long lost love.*

**LI**
You did your job well. But, this girl. . . I saw her last night.

**YU**
I knew she would intrigue you.

**LI**
She needs direction. . . and training.

**YU**
She's an aristocrat's daughter. She's not one of us. In any case, it will all be over soon. You'll kill Fox, and she'll marry.

**LI**
That's not for her. She should come to Wudan and become a disciple.

**YU**
But Wudan does not accept women.

**LI**
For her, they might make an exception. If not, I'm afraid she'll become a poisoned dragon.

**YU**
It's not our affair. Even if Wudan accepts her, her husband might object.

**LI**
I thought by giving away the sword, I could escape the Giang Hu world. But the cycle of bloodshed continues.

**YU**
I wish there were something more I could do to help you.

**LI**
Just be patient with me, Shu Lien.

**INT. JEN'S ROOM - NIGHT**
Jen is asleep. A noise awakens her.

Lo opens the window and sneaks in—right into the point of Jen's waiting sword.

Jen's sword drops to the ground.

**JEN**
Lo?

**LO**
Jen!

*FLASHBACK:*

*We go back in time to a scene in the desert. A younger Jen is riding in a carriage with her mother, with warriors surrounding the carriage for protection. Suddenly, the carriage is surrounded by bandits led by Lo. Lo reaches in through the window of the carriage and snatches Jen's jade comb from her hand. Without hesitation, Jen races after him on horseback. When Jen catches up with Lo, they fight until she collapses from thirst and hunger. She wakes in his den. He is kind and gives her food and water. But Jen's temper still rages. She hits him on the head with a rock and runs off again. Hours later, lost and exhausted, she collapses again. When she wakes she finds herself weak and dehydrated in Lo's bed. He nurses her back to health, and when she tries to fight him again they fall into an embrace.*

Lo and Jen begin a passionate love affair.
They live happily and freely in the desert
for a while. But Governor Yu's men are
looking for Jen. Lo tells her she should
return to her parents and he will earn
their respect and come for her, so they can
be married with her parents' blessing.
He tells her the legend of a boy who
jumped from a mountain they gaze
upon so that his wish would be
granted. His parents were ill, and he
jumped to save them. The boy didn't die,
and wasn't even hurt. He just floated
away on the clouds, never to return.
He knew that his wish had come true.
Lo assures Jen that they will be
together someday with the Han saying
"A faithful heart makes wishes come
true." Jen gives Lo her Jade comb
and tells him to return it to her
when they are together again.

Lo grabs her by the waist.

**JEN**
You shouldn't have come.

**LO**
With all the traffic on your rooftop these days. . . it took me a while to get in here. I can't wait any longer. I was wrong to let you go.  Come back with me. You'll be happy in the desert. You'll be free there.

Jen turns back to him and rests herself briefly in his arms again.

**JEN**
You've been looking for me all this time?

**FLASHBACK: FOUR YEARS EARLIER**

**INT./EXT. CARRIAGE/MONGOLIAN DESERT - DAY**

Jen holds up a comb, with daylight shining through it. Jen admires the piece, her most prized possession.

Madam Yu sits opposite her.

**MADAME YU**
Jen. . . stop playing with it.

Jen looks out over the desert, as the wind picks up and the sky darkens.

**JEN**
I won't break it.

**EXT. CARRIAGE/MONGOLIAN
DESERT - DAY**
Lo and a group of armed bandits
descend on the caravan.

> **GUARD A**
> It's Dark Cloud! Dark Cloud is
> coming!

His warning is useless. From Jen's pov,
we see the guards slaughtered in a hail
of arrows and swords.

> **MADAM YU**
> Lower the shade, don't let them
> see you!

> **DARK CLOUD (LO)**
> Don't touch the women!

Though unharmed, Madam Yu immediately faints. Lo approaches the carriage
and grabs the comb from Jen's hand.

She bolts from the carriage, and, once
outside, bends down and grabs a lance
from the body of a dead guard, whose
horse flails beside him.

She looks up to see the gang of
bandits already making their escape
on horseback.

> **LO**
> Let's go!

**EXT. DESERT - DAY**
Jen and Lo ride across the desert
floor at breakneck speed.

# THE GOBI DESERT

We were out in the Gobi Desert,
the hottest, driest place on earth.
So each morning we lit incense for
good luck. Well, we had dreadful
luck. It rained sheets, nonstop,
ruining our schedule. After a while
one of the local people came
around and said the gods must be
smiling on us. We asked why.
"Because you burn incense,"
he said. "We burn incense
when we want it to rain."

—BILL KONG, producer

LO
Come get your comb.

She tries to jab him with the lance, but
he grabs it and flings her off her horse.

LO
Hurry back to your mother.

Lo rides on as she charges after her
horse.

EXT. DESERT BLUFF - DAY
A group of bandits is dividing up the loot, as Jen rides up, keeping a respectable distance. They notice her and rise as she dismounts.

One of them saunters over to her and stands, grinning, a few feet away.

In a second, she's slammed his balls into his stomach and knocked his nose into his face. He crumples to the sand.

The other bandits stop laughing, quickly exchange glances, and charge her at once.

In a matter of seconds, they're either on the ground or dragging their fallen comrades back.

Lo calls out and stops the fight.

LO
She's mine.

EXT. DESERT - DAY
Lo and Jen ride, if not side-by-side, then parallel, about 20 feet apart. Their pace has slowed considerably. In fact, they're dead tired.

LO
Let's stop a moment.

JEN
Give it back!

# WORKING WITH FIGHT CHOREOGRAPHER YUEN WO PING

Yuen Wo Ping is one of my heroes. When it comes to fight sequences, Yuen is, in my opinion, without equal. It was Yuen's choreography that helped establish some of the biggest Hong Kong action heroes, like Jet Li in Tsui Hark's *Once Upon a Time in China* and Jackie Chan in *Snake Under Eagle Shadow*. Western audiences will be familiar with some of his choreography in *The Matrix*, though his work there shows only a small part of his skill.

Yuen is a master of providing thrills for the audience. He knows everything about Chinese kung fu action scenes. But he's also very cultured. He has a lot of respect for the classical martial arts style. And also the tradition of Chinese Opera, with its stylized movements and acrobatics. This is maybe where the real roots of the kung fu film are. Because of his skill and knowledge, in Yuen's choreography, the martial art becomes a peforming art.

Choreographers like Yuen Wo Ping are true filmmakers. The fight sequences that they create are not about beating someone up, or a kind of health exercise. It's really all about an energetic cinematic language. Our collaboration was beneficial for the entire film. Working with Yuen was a great inspiration for me—not only for film action, but for my filmmaking as a whole.

—ANG LEE

*Yuen Wo Ping*

## SHOOTING SCHEDULE

We started shooting in the Gobi Desert. That night, the crew got lost in the desert and it wasn't until 7 AM that we found them. We delayed shooting until 2 PM. After the second shot, a sandstorm came in. We shot around the clock with two teams. I didn't take one break in eight months, not even for half a day. I was miserable—I just didn't have the extra energy to be happy.

Near the end, I could hardly breathe; I thought I was about to have a stroke. It was bad. Six months later, I'm still resting now, trying to get fit again. But since I'm middle-aged, I'll probably never come back to normal.

—ANG LEE

**LO**
(*shouting a bit*)
You're tired. You need rest. Your horse needs water. There's a creek up here.

He dismounts, looks down at the dry creek bed.

**LO**
Well, there used to be! What's your name? I'm Lo. The Hans call me Dark Cloud. I'm not that tall or big, but I'm quick as lightning.

**JEN**
My comb!

She kicks him. They fight ferociously until Lo, exhausted, collapses. She kicks him a few times, then collapses too.

**INT. CAVE - DAY**
Jen comes to and finds herself wrapped in a blanket of animal fur. She sits up with a start and checks her clothes. Looking around, she realizes she's in a cave. Next to her are a lamp, some hunting equipment, and a neat row of sharp arrows. She quickly grabs one of the arrows.

**LO**
If you like that arrow, I can make you a bow. Great for hunting wild chicken. They're delicious.

Jen raises one of the arrows, going on the attack again, but her legs betray her and she falls.

**LO**
You need to eat, understand? Then you'll have the strength to fight. Understand?

He helps her up, then pours her some horse milk from a sac. He hands her a small chunk of food, which she first accepts grudgingly, then, her hunger getting the better of her, she starts to wolf it down.

LO

You're eating too fast. Slowly.

**EXT. CAVE - DAY**
Lo walks out into a barren mountain landscape. A chicken roasts over a fire. Lo whistles.

Jen appears suddenly with a rock and knocks it over his head. Lo passes out as Jen scurries away.

**EXT. MOUNTAINSIDE AND DESERT - DAY**
Jen tries to find her way among the treacherous stony terrain, her lips chapped and fingers bloody and blistered. But soon she passes out.

**INT. CAVE - NIGHT**
Jen again awakes inside the cave. Lo tries to feed her some water, but she chokes, and tries to push him away, only to find that her legs and hands are tied up.

LO

You've got quite a temper. It's better this way.

**JEN**

You coward!

**LO**

Still in a bad mood? At least you're speaking. What's your name?

Jen spits at Lo.

**LO**

I didn't think the Hans had names like that.

Later: She weaves in and out of consciousness. In the flickering lights, she sees Lo sharpening his arrows.

Later, he pulls back an opaque curtain to reveal a makeshift bathroom—a water-filled cavity serves as a tub.

He rises as Jen sobs at the sight of her imprisoned and dishevelled body. He comes over and unties her.

**LO**

Relax. If I had wanted to, I would already have done it. You must be dying for a bath. Fresh water's hard to get here. But I managed to bring some up. You can wear my clothes when you're done. They're clean. Don't worry. I'll sing, so you'll know where I am. After the bath, you'll be calmer.

Jen nods and the bandit releases her. He starts to sing as he walks out. Jen waits until the sound recedes before closing the curtain behind her and dipping into the pit. While she bathes, she listens to his singing, a loud rendition of a tribal song. Lo apparently doesn't remember all the lyrics, and la-las his way through more than a few passages. Jen smiles.

INT. CAVE - NIGHT

Jen grimaces as Lo pulls the last of some cactus needles from the soles of her feet.

**LO**

No more hitting on the head! All this trouble for a comb?

**JEN**

It's mine. It means a lot to me. A barbarian like you wouldn't understand.

**LO**

Not true. I can use it to pick fleas from my horse.

**JEN**

By the way, I'm a real Manchurian.

**LO**

I'm sorry. . . I guessed wrong. I thought you were a Han.

**JEN**
Give me back my comb.

**LO**
I don't take orders from anyone.

**JEN**
Give it back.

Jen impulsively grabs an arrow and stabs Lo, drawing a little blood from his chest. Furious, Lo lunges at her and they tussle briefly. Finally, Lo gets on top of Jen, and the scuffling becomes more like foreplay. Violence turns into unleashed passion.

**EXT. DESERT OASIS - DAY**
Lo and Jen ride across the desert. Jen holds tightly to him.

**EXT. CAVE - NIGHT**
Lo and Jen lie in the bath together.

**LO**
When I was a boy, one night, I saw a thousand shooting stars. I thought, where did they all go? I'm an orphan. I used to look for stars alone. I thought if I rode to the other end of the desert, I'd find them. I've been riding in the desert ever since.

**JEN**
And so, the little boy became a fearsome bandit. He couldn't find the stars, so he stole my comb.

Lo pauses.

**LO**

Out here, you always fight for
survival. You have to be part of a
gang to stand a chance. Slowly,
your gang becomes your family.
All that Dark Cloud stuff is just to
scare people and make my life
easier.

**JEN**

So you're still that little boy
looking for shooting stars.

**LO**

I am a man. And now I've found
the brightest star of all.

**EXT. DESERT - DAY**

Lo sees uniformed men through his
binoculars.

**LO**

Your father's men are looking
for you.

Jen doesn't respond.

**EXT. DESERT - DAY**

Lo and Jen ride through a mountain pass.

**EXT. CLIFF - DAY**

Lo and Jen stand at the crest of a cliff.
Lo looks over, viewing the desert valley
below, as Jen joins him. They see a
troop of uniformed men riding by in
the distance.

**LO**

Your father's men are still looking
for you. They're still out there,
circling closer.

**JEN**

Let them look.

**LO**

It is trouble for me.

Jen bites her lip.

**JEN**

Don't send me back!

**LO**

You must decide. You might get
tired of this life. You might begin
to miss your family. If it were our
daughter, we'd look for her too.
She would miss us. Jen. . . I want
you to be mine forever. I will make
my mark on the world. I will earn
your parents' respect. We have a
legend. Anyone who dares to jump
from the mountain, God will grant
his wish. Long ago, a young man's
parents were ill, so he jumped. He
didn't die. He wasn't even hurt. He
floated away, far away, never to
return. He knew his wish had
come true. If you believe, it will
happen. The elders say, "A faithful
heart makes wishes come true."

"A

FAITHFUL

HEART

MAKES

WISHES

COME

TRUE,"

> *In Jen's bedroom, Lo tells her that he tried and tried to become respectable but he was always recognized as the bandit Dark Cloud. He begs her not to marry, and to return with him to the desert. Jen tells Lo to leave and never come back. Lo returns the jade comb to Jen and leaves.*
>
> *At Jen's bridal procession the next morning, with throngs of onlookers gathered around, Lo causes a commotion shouting, "Come with me to the desert! No one marries you but me!" Governor Yu's security men chase after Lo, but Shu Lien steps in and helps him escape.*

**INT. TENT - DAY**

Jen and Lo kiss. Jen takes the jade comb out of her hair and presses it into his palm. Jen starts to cry. They embrace.

**JEN**

Keep it safe. Return it to me when we are together again.

**LO**

I will.

**JEN**
(*smiling painfully*)
If you don't, I'll come after you. And I won't let you off so easy.

**EXT. TENT - DAY**

Jen quietly walks out and stands sadly in the early morning light.

End of flashback.

**INT. JEN'S ROOM - NIGHT**

**LO**

Wherever I went, someone always recognized me. I really tried. Later, I heard you came to Peking. I was afraid I'd never see you again. So I came. I can't let you marry.

Jen is about to respond when a servant's voice is heard from outside the door.

# NO ONE MARRIES YOU BUT ME!

**JEN**
(*whispering*)
Go.

**LO**
Jen. . .

**JEN**
(*through her tears*)
Don't ever come back.

Lo hovers at the window frame

**LO**
So it's over?

Jen pauses.

**JEN**
Yes.

Lo thrusts a small object in her hand.

He lifts his legs through the window, and drops out of sight, just as Jen's door is opened from the hall.

**MAID**
We heard noises.

**JEN**
It was just a cat.

The maid pauses, then dutifully exits, closing the door.

Jen opens up her palm; gasping, she sees the comb that Lo has given her.

**EXT. WEDDING PROCESSION - DAY**
The noise and color of a wedding procession. A marching band heralds

the occasion, as throngs of onlookers fight to get a glimpse of the groom, Gou Jun Pei, who trots by on a handsome white horse.

**INT. WEDDING CARRIAGE - DAY**
Jen's head is completely covered in red cloth, as she rides silently in the bride's carriage.

**EXT. BALCONY OVERLOOKING WEDDING PROCESSION - DAY**
Li and Yu watch the festivities from a balcony of the city gate.

> YU
> You think Jade Fox will show up?

> LI
> She's out there, but I doubt she'll show herself. We'll keep our eyes open. Sooner or later, she'll come for the girl.

**INT. WEDDING CARRIAGE - DAY**
A small arrow flies into the carriage. Jen calmly lifts the red cloth from her face and pulls the arrow out of the panelling inside the carriage.

We hear Lo's voice from outside the carriage, but Jen doesn't seem to notice.

> LO
> (v.o.)
> Jen! Come with me! You're mine!

Lo runs wildly into the crowd.

> LO
> Come with me to the desert! Jen! Come with me to Xin Jiang!

The guards surround Lo, but he escapes.

**EXT. BEIJING STREET - DAY**
Lo leaps and lands right in front of Li Mu Bai, his fingers pressed against Lo's neck. Yu comes running around the corner and sees them.

**LI**

Where is Jade Fox?

Yu jumps in and pushes Li away.

**YU**

(*to Lo*)

Come with me! Hurry!

**INT. CITY OUTSKIRTS - DAY**
Lo sits dejectedly, having told his story to Yu and Li, who look him over.

**YU**

(*to Lo*)

You thought she'd give it all up and go back West with you?

**LO**

She's mine.

**LI**

Either way, you are no good to her dead. With the Gou and Yu clans hunting you, you'll soon be in their hands.

**LO**
I don't care anymore.

**LI**
If you truly loved her, you wouldn't say that.

**YU**
Don't you want to see her again.

**LI**
All right. I'll write you an introduction. Take it to Wudan. Wait there for news from me.

**LO**
All right.

**EXT. TE COMPOUND - NIGHT**
Yu and Li enter, as other men and women race through the compound, a sense of panic in the air. Yu gives Li a look. Li shrugs.

**INT. TE'S HALL - NIGHT**
A crowd, including Li and Yu, stand by as Te opens the empty sword case, his voice rising.

**SIR TE**
When will this end? They take it, they put it back, they take it again. My home is turning into a warehouse.

Bo bursts into the hall, bows to Te.

*Lo tells his story to Shu Lien and Li Mu Bai. Hearing echoes of their own thwarted love, they are sympathetic to Lo's plight and offer to help. Li sends Lo to Wudan Mountain with an introduction and tells him to wait there for news.*

*After the bridal procession, Jen disappears. And, on top of it all, the Green Destiny is stolen again, and Sir Te commissions Li and Shu Lien to find Jen and the sword.*

*Jen travels to a nearby town with the Green Destiny, masquerading as a man. Intrigued by the Green Destiny, local martial arts characters challenge Jen to fight. She swiftly defeats them one after another. After the fight, some of the men report the incident to Li Mu Bai and Shu Lien.*

**TE**
Speak!

**BO**
Jen has run away! Gou found the wedding chamber empty. Governor Yu requests your assistance. You know the Giang Hu underworld. He wants to find her, and keep her from harm.

**LI**
Sir Te, leave this to us. Don't worry.

**INT. TEA STALL - DAY**
Jen arrives at the tea stall. She places her sword on the table, which catches the attention of a couple of Giang Hu martial arts characters sitting nearby.

**WAITRESS**
What can I serve you?

As the waitress turns to leave, Jen grabs her by the arm.

**JEN**
The cup is dirty.

The flustered waitress apologizes and takes the cup away. The men approach Jen.

**GANGSTER A**
Hello. What is your name?

**JEN**
(*without lifting her eyes*)
Long.

**GANGSTER B**
It's young Master Long. My
apologies. I'm Iron Eagle Sung and
this is my brother in arms, Flying
Cougar Li Yun. What brings you
to Huai An, and where are you
headed, Master Long?

**JEN**
Anywhere there's action.

The two men exchange glances.

**GANGSTER A**
In that case, perhaps we could be
of assistance.

**JEN**
Don't bother.

**GANGSTER A**
You don't seem to understand.

**JEN**
So what if I don't?

**GANGSTER B**
We have ways of helping you
understand.

The two pull out their weapons which are immediately chopped into scraps by Jen.

**GANGSTER A**
(*stunned*)
Are you related to Li Mu Bai!?

**JEN**
He is my defeated foe!

**EXT. WOODS - DAY**
Li and Yu pass a cup back and forth as Bo tends to the horses in the background.

**YU**
Have some tea.

As Yu passes the cup to Li, their fingers touch. Embarrassed, Li pulls back.

**LI**
Shu Lien. . . The things we touch have no permanence. My master would say. . . there is nothing we can hold on to in this world. Only by letting go can we truly possess what is real.

**YU**
Not everything is an illusion. My hand. . . wasn't that real?

**LI**
Your hand, rough and callused

from machete practice. . . All this time, I've never had the courage to touch it.

Li takes Yu's hand and presses it to his face.

**LI**
Giang Hu is a world of tigers and dragons, full of corruption. . . I tried sincerely to give it up but I have brought us only trouble.

**YU**
To repress one's feelings only makes them stronger.

**LI**
You're right, but I don't know what to do. I want to be with you. . . just like this. It gives me a sense of peace.

Li Mu Bai smiles.

**INT. STAR RESTAURANT - DAY**
Jen walks upstairs. A waiter greets her.

**WAITER**
Please follow me.

**JEN**
I want a clean room.

**WAITER**
We have plenty. Your order?

Jen again sets her sword on the table as she sits down.

**JEN**
Steamed whole cod, bite-size meat-balls, a little starchy, but keep the sauce light, shark fin soup, mixed vegetables, and some warm wine.

**WAITER**
(*dazed*)
I have to order from a bigger restaurant.

**JEN**
Hurry then.

The waiter gauges Jen for an instant before bouncing off to place the orders. Jen checks her pouch and sees there's not much money left.

A large group of Giang Hu characters enters. They survey the restaurant and quickly find Jen upstairs.

**GIANG HU A**
That's him.

**MI BIAO**
I am Iron Arm Mi. I heard a true master has arrived. I have come to seek a lesson.

Jen ignores him.

**MI BIAO**
(*bristles*)
You asked for it!

Mi charges and attacks Jen, who is still sitting sipping tea. Jen barely lifts a finger and disposes of Mi with a poke at a sensitive pressure point. This provokes a reaction from the other men.

**JEN**
What kind of Iron Arm are you?

**FLYING MACHETE CHANG**
You have amazing technique! I am Flying Machete. Are you related to Southern Crane?

**JEN**
Southern Duck? I don't eat any-thing with two feet. Who could remember such long-winded names?

**GOU JUN SIHUNG**
Li Mu Bai is your defeated foe, and you don't know his master, Southern Crane?

**JEN**
Who are you?

**GOU JUN SIHUNG**
I'm Shining Phoenix Mountain Gou.

## ABOUT WUXIA PIAN

*A xia* is a knight-errant, who might come from any class, and *wuxia* involves knightly chivalry. The Chinese concept of the knight-errant originates in the fourth century B.C., but chivalric stories as we know them today go back to the Tang dynasty, around the ninth century A.D. Some were literary efforts composed by men of learning, others were oral tales and ballads in colloquial prose or simple verse. By the seventeenth century, these forms had become a flourishing fictional genre concentrating on vagabond warriors who display outstanding courage, honor, and fighting skills. Magical elements had also entered the mix, so knights were often given superhuman powers—flying, hurling balls of fire, becoming invisible. Many stories played on the boundary between pure fantasy and what might be barely possible for a supremely trained and gifted warrior—not really flying but the "weightless leap"; not being invulnerable but being able, through control of breathing, to make one's body as hard as iron. To enjoy the *wuxia* tale we must grant that supreme skill in martial arts could give a fighter extraordinary powers.

—DAVID BORDWELL

**JEN**

(*furious*)

Gou? I hate that name. It makes me puke! Too bad you're named Gou. You'll be the first to feel my sword today.

Jen leaps up and dives into battle. The men all use different kinds of weapons, but they all succumb to the powerful Green Destiny.

**MONK JING**

Hold it! Don't you know Monk Jing?

**JEN**

A monk, in a place like this? You need a lesson!

**MONK JING**

Who are you?

She smiles, and leaps again into action after unsheathing the Green Destiny.

**JEN**

Who am I? I am. . . I am the Invincible Sword Goddess. Armed with the incredible. . . Green Destiny. Be you Li or Southern Crane. . . lower your head. . . and ask for mercy. I am the desert dragon. I leave no trace. Today I fly over Eu-Mei. Tomorrow. . . I'll kick over Wudan Mountain!

Jen is in a frenzy, slashing and maiming as she speaks.

*When Shu Lien returns to her compound to prepare to search for Jen, Jen shows up on her doorstep calling Shu Lien her sister and begging for guidance. Shu Lien comforts her and advises her to return to her parents, then decide about Lo. When Jen learns that Shu Lien has partnered with Li Mu Bai to track her down, she becomes suspicious and tries to leave. Shu Lien tries to stop Jen and a battle begins between the two women. Shu Lien uses every weapon in her arsenal but the Green Destiny is too powerful.*

**INT. STAR RESTAURANT - DAY**
Yu and Li are surrounded by the variously bandaged men who battled with Jen.

**FLYING MACHETE CHANG**
We politely asked for a friendly match, but she showed no respect, and attacked us. Everyone came by to teach her a lesson.

**MI BIAO**
Her sword was just too powerful.

**MONK JING**
I've traveled everywhere, but never met anyone so uncivilized.

**SHINING PHOENIX MOUNTAIN GOU**
(*heavily bandaged*)
She kept accusing me of being Gou Jun Pei's brother. Who is this Gou, anyway?

**YU**
Her husband.

The men all nod their heads.

**EXT. OUTSIDE HWAI AN - DAY**
Li and Yu ride together.

**LI**
(*to Yu*)
We're close to your headquarters. Go home and check in.

**YU**
What about you?

**LI**
I'll look around and catch up later.

**YU**
Not a bad idea. Tonight we'll get a good night's sleep at headquarters.

Yu takes a fork off the road. Thunder can be heard in the darkening sky.

**EXT. SUN COMPOUND - DAY**
A group of security men are practicing Kung Fu in the front yard of Sun Security. They stop when Yu enters.

**SECURITY MAN A**
Mistress, you're back.

**YU**
It's you! How's everything here?

**CAPTAIN**
Fine. You've been gone a while.

**YU**
Yes, and I leave again tomorrow. Your wife was due?

**AH WAI**
Yeah, a baby girl.

**YU**
Good!

# FILMMAKING

My desire to direct a martial arts film comes from nostalgia for classical China. The greatest appeal of the kung-fu world lies in its abstractions. It is a conceptual world based on "imaginary China." This world does not exist in reality and is therefore free from its constraints. Here, I can express sentimentality; action scenes play like choreographed dances. I can design music and sound effects. There are no limitations. It is a free and unrestrained form of filmmaking.

—ANG LEE

**AH WAI**
I'll be happy if she's half as strong as you.

**YU**
Mrs. Wu. . .

**AUNT WU**
You're back!

**YU**
How's the arm? Still sore?

**AUNT WU**
Much better. You've been gone so long.

**YU**
Li Mu Bai is coming to stay the night.

**AUNT WU**
(*excited*)
I'll go and make up his room!

Aunt Wu hustles out. Yu goes into her own room.

**INT. HALL OF ANCESTRAL WORSHIP**
Yu lights incense for her former fiancé Meng. Hearing something, she turns to see a dishevelled Jen standing outside downstairs.

**JEN**
Sister Shu Lien. . .

**INT. YU'S ROOM - DAY**
Yu eases her guard, then opens a drawer, and takes out some clothes. Jen, wearing just white underclothing, sets herself on the edge of Yu's bed. Yu brings over the clothes.

**YU**
Here you must be in proper attire.

**JEN**
I'm just borrowing some clean clothes. I'm not staying.

**YU**
I'll give them to you.

JEN
I was just passing by and
wondered how you were.

Jen tries to hide her anxiety but finally
breaks down on Yu's shoulder in tears.

JEN
You, sister. . .

YU
Look at the trouble you've caused.
Now you know what Giang Hu life
is really like. If you think of me as
your sister, let me give you some
sisterly advice. You can run from
marriage, but not your parents.

JEN
They forced me to marry!

YU
Go back to them first. Then you
can decide about Lo.

JEN
You know about Lo?

YU
He really loves you. Come back to
Peking with me. We'll find a
solution.

JEN
Where is he now?

YU
Li Mu Bai has made arrangements.
He sent him to Wudan Mountain.

JEN
You're working together to set me
up! I'm leaving!

YU
How dare you accuse us? I always
knew you had stolen the sword!
I've done nothing but protect you
and your family. And you've repaid
me with nothing but contempt. Li
Mu Bai himself spared you, and all
you do is insult him. We wanted
some peace and you've ruined it
all! You're no sister of mine!

JEN
What do I care? You were never a
real friend anyway. But I wonder,
how long could you last as my
enemy?

Jen gets up to leave. Yu intercepts her.

YU
Put the sword down!

Jen jumps out.

INT. YUAN COURTYARD - DAY
Jen soars out to the front courtyard
where the guards are still practicing.

They raise their weapons at the sight of an intruder.

>            **YU**
>       (*calling out*)
>       Jen!

Jen greets Yu with the Green Destiny.

>            **YU**
>       Everyone out. Shut the doors.

The men leave.

>            **YU**
>       Fine. . . the friendship is over.

Yu scoops up a weapon from one of

FINE . . .

THE

FRIENDSHIP

IS

OVER.

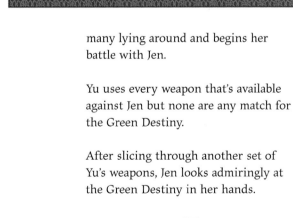

*As Jen is about to defeat her, Li rushes in and saves Shu Lien. As they fight, Li makes his offer to train Jen at Wudan again. Jen presents a challenge—if Li can take the sword from her in three moves, she will be his pupil. Li succeeds, but Jen reneges on their deal. Li throws the Green Destiny into the rushing rapids below and Jen dives after it.*

many lying around and begins her battle with Jen.

Yu uses every weapon that's available against Jen but none are any match for the Green Destiny.

After slicing through another set of Yu's weapons, Jen looks admiringly at the Green Destiny in her hands.

**YU**
Don't touch it! That's Li Mu Bai's sword.

**JEN**
Come and get it if you can.

**YU**
Without the Green Destiny, you are nothing.

**JEN**
Don't be a sore loser. Go ahead. Take your pick. I'll wait. Go ahead.

Yu picks up a huge broad sword and attacks. Just as the Green Destiny slices it in half, Yu holds the broken blade at Jen's neck. She pauses before hurting Jen, then pulls back.

**YU**
Give me the sword.

Jen, taking advantage of Yu's trust, slices her arm.

**JEN**
Take it!

Yu, her shoulder bleeding, falls back as Li Mu Bai jumps in.

**LI**
(*enraged*)
Stop it! You don't deserve the Green Destiny.

**JEN**
Not another lecture! On guard!

**LI**
Let's end this here.

**JEN**
Only the sword will settle this.

Jen soars up to the rooftop, with Li right on her tail.

**EXT. LAKE - DAY**
Jen floats over the lake, Li close behind.

**EXT. BAMBOO FOREST - DAY**
Jen runs into a sea of bamboo. She appears to have lost Li but is not slowing down. Her white clothes are now stained with blood and mud. The wind had picked up and every breeze sounds like an air attack by Li.

The two leap onto the tips of the bamboo trees and begin their dances and dodges. They glance off bamboos and each other while staying afloat. Finally Jen lands on the same stick of bamboo as Li. The two hold their positions for a while, as the bamboo bends.

**LI**
I only let you go because I wanted to see the real you.

Jen tries to shake Li off the bamboo but Li recovers nicely.

**JEN**
What do you know about a true heart?

# IN THE
# BAMBOO TREES

In King Hu's *A Touch of Zen* (1971), the knights prudently do battle under bamboo trees. Lee had the inspired—or crackpot—idea to stage the fight between Mubai and Jen on the trees' branches. Says Zhang: "I had to swing up and down, swirl, and remember to try and act, all at the same time." Chow was grateful to the action director: "Wo Ping gave me as much protection as he could. He knows I'm not a martial arts man. And when you're hanging 60 feet up in the air in a bamboo forest, you need protection."

When he thinks about the scene, Lee is both chagrined and giddy. "It's nuts," he says. "It's sexy. Nobody wanted to do it. And there's a reason why people don't do that: because it's almost impossible! The first three days of shooting we did were a complete waste of time. There were 20 or 30 guys below the actors trying to make them float. It was just chaotic." Finally it worked: a scene so buoyant that the audience roars and soars along with the stars.

—RICHARD CORLISS

I supervised 300 wire-removals, sky replacement, and the coloring of the entire bamboo sequence on the computer during post-production in Hong Kong. Leo Lo and his team at Asia Cine Digital only slept four to five hours a night for about seventy days to meet the deadline for Cannes. Some of the most difficult wire-removal shots in the bamboo sequence took two months to complete due to thousands of leaves moving in the background.

—PETER PAU, Director of Photography

Li suddenly leaps off the bamboo tree. The bamboo straightens up and throws Jen toward the ground. Jen quickly pulls herself up and charges at Li.

Jen chases after Li, into a clearing, out of the bamboo forest.

**EXT. RIVER - DAY**
Jen finally catches up to Li, who is standing on a rock about a few feet wide amid the rapids. Jen vaults onto the rock and scuffles with Li. Jen loses her balance.

> **JEN**
> What do you want?

> **LI**
> What I've always wanted, to teach you.

> **JEN**
> All right. If you can take back the sword in three moves, I'll go with you.

Li takes the sword back.

> **JEN**
> Give it back!

> **LI**
> Kneel!

> **JEN**
> Never!

> **LI**
> Then you have no use for the sword.

Li throws the sword into the rapids.

*Jen is knocked unconscious and nearly drowns, but Jade Fox rescues her. Jen awakes, confused, in an abandoned kiln. Jade Fox declares that she and Jen will stick together from now on and leaves Jen alone clutching the Green Destiny. Jen awakes flushed with fever. Li Mu Bai arrives and expels the poison from her body. Shu Lien and Bo arrive, having tracked Jade Fox back to the abandoned kiln. Jade Fox suddenly appears, shooting a flurry of poison arrows. Li deflects most of the arrows, but one hits his neck. Li kills Jade Fox, but the damage has already been done. The poison is already in his bloodstream. Jen knows the antidote and offers to save Li as he saved her. She races to Shu Lien's compound to obtain the antidote.*

Jen dives in to retrieve it. He follows Jen downstream by hopping from one rock to another. Jen recovers the sword but is herself drowning. Suddenly Jade Fox swings into the rapids and fishes Jen out. Jade Fox carries the unconscious Jen away. Li gives chase, but loses them.

**INT. ABANDONED FACTORY - DAY**
It's raining. Inside an old factory, Fox heats some medicine paste and then dips a needle in the paste. She burns the needle point, causing a blue smoke. She lights some incense and puts it in a burner near Jen, who is barely conscious.

> **FOX**
> Sooner or later, they'd drag you back to Peking. Your parents will never accept you again. But why go home? We've gone this far, we won't stop now. You'll always be my lady. At last, we'll be our own masters. We'll be happy. That's the most important thing. All we have left is each other, right? Lie down and rest.

Jen is too weak to respond.

Fox leaves Jen clutching the Green Destiny.

**EXT. ABANDONED FACTORY - DAY**
Fox scurries ahead in the rain. Her eyes catch something, but she keeps moving.

**INT. YUAN COMPOUND - DAY**
Aunt Wu finishes bandaging Yu.

>                    **AUNT WU**
>       She's crazy. You should have killed
>       her.

>                    **YU**
>       I didn't have the heart.

>                    **AUNT WU**
>       Well, Li Mu Bai can do it.

Yu senses movement at the window.
Looking out, she sees Jade Fox in the
distance.

**INT. ABANDONED FACTORY - DAY**
Jen wakes up, flushed from fever. She takes a sip from a cup of water—it's empty. She tosses the cup, gets up, and walks into the rain.

**EXT. ABANDONED FACTORY - DAY**
Jen walks out, raises her face into the rain, and drinks the raindrops. Thirst quenched, she turns around and finds Li standing there. Jen limps towards him while mumbling.

>                    **JEN**
>       Is it me or the sword you want?

Jen falls into Li, who checks her pulse and looks at her eyes.

>                    **LI**
>       You've been drugged!

# CO-WRITING THE SCREENPLAY

**JAMES SCHAMUS:** We came to the script originally with a very strong narrative focus—breathless storytelling of a really fun kind. But when the script was translated from English to Chinese, it was clear that there was a lot of the culture that was missing in the original English script—because we weren't focused on how the texture, both verbally in the language as well as physically in the way the people related to each other, was going to make its way into the movie.

So there was a very, very big rewrite done on the picture by Wang Hui Ling, a writer based in Taiwan. When we translated that back, I was able to ingest an enormous amount of information in detail and feelings, which I never had before. Then we backed into the script to restructure it into a more western narrative form.

The back-and-forth of these two approaches really accelerated as we got into production. I was literally commuting back and forth to China, writing scenes.

**ANG LEE:** Between all of the different writers, I was the guy who was in the middle, who was in between the two worlds.

**JAMES SCHAMUS:** English is only a few hundred years old. I am reading *Beowulf* right now, which is about 1200 years old, and even it has to be translated into contemporary English to be understood. When somebody says something in this film, the Chinese character that is written down, that attaches to that, has roots that are 5,000 years old, if not older. The Chinese embedded in every word of this movie has layers and layers of culture and meanings. They simply don't exist to a Western ear. It is one of the truly delicious ironies of this movie that although I co-wrote it, I'll never fully understand all of its meanings.

*Right: James Schamus.*
*Above: Ang Lee.*

Li carries her inside, kicking away the incense burner.

**INT. ABANDONED FACTORY - DAY**
Li lays his hands on Jen's back; she slowly comes to.

**LI**
Where is Jade Fox?

Jen gestures that she doesn't know. Yu and Bo enter. Yu looks at Jen.

**YU**
What happened?

**LI**
Jade Fox drugged her. How did you get here?

**YU**
We followed Jade Fox.

Instantaneously, a flurry of darts flies directly in Jen's direction. Li and Yu swipe miraculously at them all, sending them flinging hither and thither.

Fox shows herself. Li attacks her. She falls back, bleeding to death.

**LI**
And so you die.

Li touches his neck.

**FOX**
And so shall you!

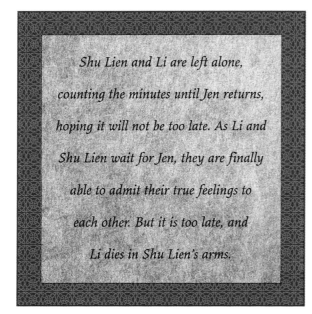

*Shu Lien and Li are left alone, counting the minutes until Jen returns, hoping it will not be too late. As Li and Shu Lien wait for Jen, they are finally able to admit their true feelings to each other. But it is too late, and Li dies in Shu Lien's arms.*

Li pulls a single needle from his neck.

**YU**
A poisoned needle!

**FOX**
You deserve to die, but the life I was hoping to take. . . was Jen's. Ten years I devoted to you. But you deceived me! You hid the manual's true meaning. I never improved. . . but your progress was limitless! You know what poison is? An eight-year-old girl, full of deceit. That's poison! Jen! My only family. . . my only enemy. . .

Jade Fox dies.

**YU**
You can't die! Tell us what poison you used! You can't die! Tell us the antidote! You can't let Li Mu Bai die!

**JEN**
She used Purple Yin. . . Purple Yin poison. It goes straight to the heart.

**LI**
My blood will soon reverse its flow. It's the same poison she used to kill my master. There is no antidote.

**YU**
That can't be! Everything has an antithesis! Why not this?

**JEN**
The antidote exists. She taught it to me. The formula is simple, but it takes time to prepare. Trust me. As you have helped me, let me help him.

**LI**
All right. Hurry. I will hold on as long as I can.

**YU**
(*takes the comb from her hair*)
Take my horse and go to the compound. Give this to Mrs. Wu. She'll help you. Hurry!

**JEN**
Spare your energy. I'll be back!

**EXT. ABANDONED FACTORY - NIGHT**
Bo is burying Fox in the rain.

**EXT. YUAN COMPOUND - NIGHT**
The guards surround Jen. She pushes
past them.

**JEN**
Where is Mrs. Wu?

Aunt Wu comes running out.

**AUNT WU**
Stop it!

Jen pulls out Yu's comb.

**JEN**
Shu Lien told me to show you this.

**AUNT WU**
Let her in.

**INT. ABANDONED FACTORY - NIGHT**
Yu sits across from Li, whose pose is
almost meditational, eerily calm.

**YU**
Mu Bai, hold on. Give me some
hope. . .

**LI**
Shu Lien. . .

**YU**
Save your strength.

# BECAUSE OF YOUR LOVE . . . I WILL NEVER BE A LONELY SPIRIT.

**LI**
My life is departing. I've only one breath left.

**YU**
Use it to meditate. Free yourself from this world as you have been taught. Let your soul rise to eternity with your last breath. Do not waste it. . . for me.

**LI**
I've already wasted my whole life. I want to tell you with my last breath. . . I have always loved you. I would rather be a ghost, drifting by your side. . . as a condemned soul. . . than enter heaven without you. Because of your love. . . I will never be a lonely spirit.

Yu cries.

She kisses him lightly. He closes his eyes.

**EXT. PATH - DAY**
As the sun rises, Jen rides speedily, clutching the medicine in her hands.

**INT. ABANDONED FACTORY - DAY**
Li is in Yu's arms. They're holding hands. The sun shines in. Yu slowly releases Li's stiff fingers—he is dead.

Jen is at the door.

**JEN**
He's gone?

Bo peeks over Jen's shoulder.

Yu rises and picks up Green Destiny. Jen kneels. Yu raises the sword, but doesn't kill her.

**YU**
Bo. . . please take this sword back to Sir Te.

He takes the sword from her.

**YU**
(to Jen)
Now you must go to Wudan

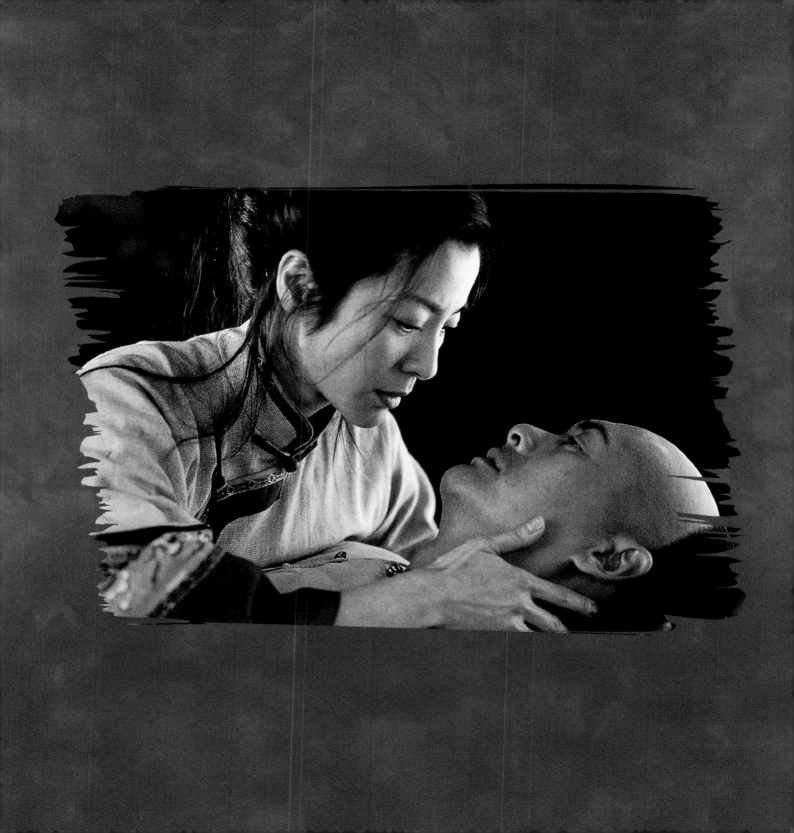

# THE WUXIA ACCORDING TO ANG LEE

The *Wuxia* is a particularly Chinese type of hero (or heroine). *Wu* means martial, and a rough equivalent for *xia* in Western culture would be knight-errant. Unlike the knight-errant, however, the *Wuxia* is a free spirit, not belonging to any class. In the world of the *Wuxia*, the most important values are honor, loyalty, and individual justice.

These qualities became ideals, and the *Wuxia* became a mythical, larger than life hero in the Chinese imagination. By the Ching Dynasty, in the eighteenth and the nineteenth centuries, *Wuxia* fiction was very popular. The story of the *Wuxia* became a fantasy of power, romance, and moral duty—embodied by Li Mu Bai and Shu Lien in *Crouching Tiger*.

As the genre developed, the *Wuxia* character became a more independent figure, often serving the basic principles of honor and justice themselves, rather than a particular master. In this respect, the *Wuxia* is not unlike the familiar Western hero—the lone cowboy riding into town to exact justice and right wrongs.

The world of the *Wuxia* is different from that of society. The *Wuxia* operates in a realm under the surface of society and the rule of law, called *Giang Hu*. This is a world made up of individuals and their relationships, rather than the collective and the government. These relationships can exist entirely outside of the law. For example, the *Wuxia* can be a member of an underground, Mafia-type organization, but loyalty and honor are still the main values. In serving a master, the *Wuxia* keeps his or her word, even to the point of death. (Today, the term *Giang Hu* has a broader meaning, referring to the entanglements of life and relationships in a society.)

The fictional *Giang Hu* world is very popular in Chinese culture. Li Mu Bai's character—righting wrongs, staying true to his word—is wishful thinking come true. A constant theme of the *Wuxia* novels is that of surpassing your abilities through practicing your martial art. You keep doing this, and fulfill the final achievement, which is transcendence.

Li Mu Bai practices the Wudan style of martial arts. In the popular imagination of *Wuxia* stories, a distinction is made between this and the Shaolin style of martial arts. The more violent *Shaolin* stands for outer strength, while *Wudan*—the style of Li Mu Bai—signifies inner strength. In fact, the two styles have a common origin in the efforts of ordinary Chinese to defend themselves from danger. Fighting eventually became the province of the military, and was further refined and codified into the Chinese martial arts. The disciplines of *Wudan* and *Shaolin* are not separate or opposite. In Chinese philosophy as a whole—and not just martial arts—inner and outer strength are both integral parts of every living being. Just as everyone has the Buddha within themselves, they also have a tremendous power—the crouching tiger, ready to leap out. The key is to achieve a balance, to seek harmony and reduce conflicts. Therefore to focus on real strength.

Coming from this kind of culture, stories like *Crouching Tiger* have been generally filmed in a particularly Eastern cinematic style. I have also worked in the very different Western cinematic tradition. Rather than choose between these two, I let the creative tension between these two styles became an important part of the making of *Crouching Tiger*.

## THE REAL HERO

Li Mu Bai and Yu Shu Lien are accurate portrayals of two common character stereotypes in Chinese society. They live by a Confucian moral code; they live for the community. In "Giang Hu," you need skills to survive as well as respect from the masses. Jen symbolizes their souls' desire. In fact, Jen is the real hero. Her personality is what defeats Li Mu Bai and Yu. She takes advantage of their humility. Bound by the forces of society, Li and Yu never fully enjoyed the thrills and excitement of youth. They pay dearly for their status; regrets mount as their youth fades.

—Ang Lee

Mountain. Lo awaits you there. Promise me one thing, whatever path you take in this life. . . be true to yourself.

**EXT. WU TAN TEMPLE - DAY**
Jen climbs up toward the temple, finally reaching the temple gate, and sees Lo standing there.

He runs to her. She greets him.

**INT. WU TAN TEMPLE - MAGIC**
Jen and Lo make love.

**INT. WU TAN TEMPLE - DAY**
Lo wakes up to find the jade comb on the pillow beside him, Jen gone.

**EXT. WU TAN MOUNTAIN - DAY**
Lo catches up to Jen, who stands on a

bridge. The gorges below are shrouded in clouds. She looks back at him.

> **JEN**
> Do you remember the legend of the young man?

> **LO**
> "A faithful heart makes wishes come true."

> **JEN**
> Make a wish, Lo.

Lo pauses.

> **LO**
> (*closing his eyes*)
> To be back in the desert, together again.

*Jen travels to Wudan Mountain and reunites with Lo. But there is still one unexpected and sublime act to be played out in this epic tale of love and honor . . .*

Jen smiles, turns, and leaps into the clouds. They seem to catch her gently, before she disappears into them.

Lo remains standing, a smile on his face, tears rolling down his cheeks.

THE END.

# BIOGRAPHIES

**ANG LEE** (Director/Producer) was born in Taiwan in 1954, and moved to the United States in 1978, where he received his BFA in theater from the University of Illinois and his MFA in film production from New York University. In 1983 he won the Taiwanese Golden Harvest Film Festival Best Narrative Film Award for his film "Dim Lake." While at NYU, Lee directed "Fine Line," a 45-minute film that received Best Director and Best Film at the 1985 NYU Film Festival.

"Pushing Hands," Ang Lee's first feature, was screened in the Panorama section of the 1992 Berlin Film Festival, and won Best Film in the Asian-Pacific Film Festival. It was also nominated for nine Golden Horse awards (the Taiwanese Academy Award) and won three, including a Special Jury Prize for Ang Lee's direction. In 1994, "The Wedding Banquet" premiered at the Berlin Film Festival (1993) and was awarded Berlin's top prize, the Golden Bear. The film was nominated for the Academy and Golden Globe awards for Best Foreign Language Film, and six Independent Spirit Awards. In Taiwan, "The Wedding Banquet" received five Golden Horse Awards, including awards for Best Film and Best Director. "Eat Drink Man Woman," the third film in Ang Lee's "Father Knows Best" trilogy, premiered as the opening night film in the Director's Fortnight at the Cannes Film Festival (1994). It was nominated for Academy and Golden Globe awards, and was voted Best Foreign Language Film by the National Board of Review.

In 1995, Ang Lee directed "Sense and Sensibility," starring Emma Thompson, Hugh Grant, and Kate Winslet, with a screenplay by Thompson. The film was nominated for seven Academy Awards, including Best Picture, and won the Oscar for Best Screenplay Adaptation. In addition, the film received the Golden Bear Award at the Berlin Film Festival, as well as

Golden Globes for Best Screenplay and Best Film.

In 1996, Ang Lee completed "The Ice Storm," his first feature on an entirely American subject, which was adapted from the acclaimed novel by Rick Moody, and starred Kevin Kline, Sigourney Weaver, and Joan Allen. The film was selected for competition at the 50th International Film Festival in Cannes (1997), and won the award for Best Screenplay Adaptation.

In 1999, Ang Lee directed "Ride with the Devil," a Civil War era western adapted from Daniel Woodrell's novel *Woe to Live On* by James Schamus.

**JAMES SCHAMUS** (Executive Producer and Screenwriter) founded the independent production company Good Machine with Ted Hope in 1991.

Schamus's other collaborations with Ang Lee include producing "The Ice Storm," which he also adapted from the novel by Rick Moody and which received the Best Screenplay Prize at the 1997 Cannes Film Festival, along with 1998 Writer's Guild and BAFTA nominations; writing and producing "Ride with the Devil"; co-producing "Sense And Sensibility" (Golden Bear, 1996 Berlin Film Festival, Golden Globe Award for Best Picture, Academy Award for Best Screenplay Adaptation); co-writing and associate-producing "Eat Drink Man Woman" (opening night film, Director's Fortnight, Cannes 1994, Academy Award nominee for Best Foreign Film, 1994); producing and co-writing "The Wedding Banquet" (Golden Bear, 1993 Berlin Film Festival and Academy Award nominee, Best Foreign Film, 1993); and producing Lee's first feature, "Pushing Hands."

Over the past several years, Schamus has served as executive producer on a variety of independent films, including Todd Solondz's "Happiness," Todd Haynes's "Safe," Nicole Holofcener's "Walking And Talking," Cindy Sherman's "Office Killer," Bart Freundlich's "The Myth of Fingerprints," Hannah Weyer's "Arresting Gena," Frank Grow's "Love God," and John O'Hagan's "Wonderland."

Schamus has also been involved in four of the last nine Grand Jury Prize Winners at Sundance: "The Brothers McMullen" by Edward Burns (1995, executive producer with Ted Hope); Tom Noonan's "What Happened Was . . ." (1994, executive producer with Hope); Alexandre Rockwell's "In The Soup" (1992, associate producer); and "Poison," by Todd Haynes (1991, executive producer).

Schamus is Associate Professor of film theory, history, and criticism at Columbia University, where he was recently a University Lecturer. He was also the 1997 Nuveen Fellow in the Humanities at the University of Chicago. He currently serves on the board of directors of the Foundation for Independent Video and Film, and on the board of Creative Capital.

**WANG HUI LING** (Screenwriter) co-wrote "Eat Drink Man Woman" with James Schamus, and is a successful television writer in Taiwan.

**TSAI KUO JUNG** (Screenwriter) is an acclaimed film critic in Taiwan, and chief entertainment editor of the "China Times," the most respected newspaper in Taiwan. He has written numerous television and feature film scripts as well as the books, "Chinese Movies Culture Research," and "A Dream is Gone— Hong Kong and Taiwanese Movie Star Analysis."

**BILL KONG** (Producer) is head of Edko Films Ltd., one of the longest-standing independent film companies in Hong Kong. Founded by Kong's father Kong Cho Yee in 1959 as the first Chinese-run independent film company in Hong Kong, Edko began importing and exporting movies, and building cinemas across Hong Kong. Bill assumed the responsibility from his father in the 1980s and expanded the operation of cinema-operating, film distribution, and film production. Today Edko operates one of the biggest theater circuits in Hong Kong, consisting of ten theaters. Edko distributes forty movies to the Hong Kong public every year. Edko is also a strong advocate of local movies, helping many local filmmakers get their movies made. Acclaimed filmmakers like Tsui Hark, Yim Ho, Jacob Cheung, and Ang Lee all work closely with Edko to produce local films.

**HSU LI KONG** (Producer) is one of the most important producers of modern Taiwanese cinema, and is currently President of Zoom Hunt International Productions Co. Ltd. Hsu was head of the Taiwan film archives before working for the Kuomingtong Cultural Work Committee. He then joined the central Motion Picture Corporation as General Manager and Production Chief. During his tenure at CMPC, he oversaw the production of some of the best known Taiwan films, including Ang Lee's first three films, "Pushing Hands," "The Wedding Banquet," and "Eat Drink Man Woman," as well as "Hills of No Return," "Vive L'Amour," "The Peony Pavillion," "Siao Yu," "The Accidental Legend," and "The River." Hsu left CMPC in 1997 to form Zoom Hunt International Production Co., which produces television series and films, including "Sweet Degeneration," "Love Go Go," and "The Personals." Hsu has also written numerous television scripts.

**DAVID LINDE** (Executive Producer) joined Paramount Pictures Corp. in 1985, after attending Swarthmore College. At Paramount, he supervised the sales of select international theatrical rights. In 1988, he left Paramount for an international sales position at Fox/Lorber Associates, and in 1990 he was named Vice President. At Fox/Lorber, he directed the sales of over 300 independently produced film, documentary, and television titles.

He joined Miramax Films in 1991 as Vice President of Acquisitions, where he acquired such acclaimed independent films as Chen Kaige's "Farewell My Concubine," Peter Jackson's "Heavenly Creatures," John Sayles' "Passion Fish," and Woody Allen's "Bullets over Broadway." In 1992, he was named Senior Vice President (and subsequently Executive

Vice President—Head of Sales) at the newly created Miramax International, distributor of International box office successes, such as Quentin Tarantino's "Pulp Fiction," Robert Altman's "Pret-A-Porter," Wayne Wang's "Smoke," Woody Allen's "Mighty Aphrodite," and Anthony Minghella's Academy Award–winning "The English Patient."

In January 1997, David joined Good Machine as a partner. Good Machine subsequently announced the formation of Good Machine International (GMI) with David as President. Linde executive produced Ang Lee's "Ride with the Devil," Todd Solondz's "Happiness," the CableACE Award-winning documentary "Wonderland"; and the documentaries "Guys and Dolls off the Record," "The Who's Tommy," and "The Belly Talkers." He is also serving as executive producer on Todd Solondz's next film as well as Kristian Levring's "The King Is Alive."

**PETER PAU** (Director of Photography) has been nominated for fourteen Hong Kong Film Awards for Best Cinematography, and has won three—for "The Bride with White Hair" in 1994, "Saviour of the Soul" in 1992, and "A Fishy Story" in 1990. Pau's numerous film credits as cinematographer include "Metade Fumaca," "Bride of Chucky," "Anna Magdalena," "The Phantom Lover," "The Chinese Feast," "Treasure Hunt," "Bury Me High," "The Legend of Wisely," and "The Killer." Pau also directed "Misty" and "The Temptation of Dance." He is currently serving as Director of Photography on the Golden Harvest Release "And I Hate You So."

**YUEN WO PING** (Action Choreographer) served as the Fight Choreographer for Keanu Reeves' 1999 mega-hit "The Matrix," and has collaborated with such celebrated Hong Kong martial artists as Jackie Chan, Jet Li, and Sammo Hung. Wo Ping has an extended list of film credits, in which he has taken on the role of action choreographer, director, actor, and producer.

Wo Ping was born in 1945—the eldest son

in a family of 12 in Guangzhan, China. In the 1960s, Wo Ping found work as a stuntman and kung fu fighter. By the age of 26, he had earned his first film choreography credits with the early kung fu hits of Ng See Yuen. In 1978, Wo Ping directed the well regarded "The Eagle's Shadow," starring the now legendary, international cross-over star Jackie Chan. He went on to direct another Jackie Chan feature "Drunken Master."

By 1979, Wo Ping had formed his own production and choreography company. The timing proved fortuitous, with the popularity of kung fu growing steadily in China and worldwide. Through the years, Yuen Wo Ping has worked with or directed many of China's top film talents. "Last Hero in China," "Tai Chi Master," and "Fist of Legend" featured the incomparable Jet Li, recently seen in "Lethal Weapon 4" and "Romeo Must Die." Sammo Hung, now of CBS-TV's "Martial Law," worked with Wo Ping in both "The Magnificent Butcher" and "Eastern Condors." One of Wo Ping's most highly regarded film's is 1991's "Iron Monkey," starring popular star Donnie Yen.

**TIM SQUYRES** (Editor) edited Ang Lee's films "Ride with the Devil," "The Ice Storm," "Sense and Sensibility," "Eat Drink Man Woman," and "The Wedding Banquet." His other credits include Paul Auster's "Lulu on the Bridge"; television documentaries for Bill Moyers, Michael Moore, ESPN, and VH-1; and numerous commercials and music videos.

**TIM YIP** (Production Design/Costume Design) is active in both theatrical and film production. He started his career as an Art Director in the Hong Kong film industry in the 1980s, producing a remarkable list of credits, including films by John Woo, Wayne Wang, Ringo Lam, Stanley Kwan, and Clara Law. Yip's credits include "A Better Tomorrow," "City on Fire," "Rouge," "Eat a Bowl of Rice," "The Peony Pavillion," and "Temptation of a Monk," for which he won the 1994 Golden Horse Award for Best Art Direction.

TAN DUN (Music) began his career in his native China in the Peking Opera. A graduate of Beijing's Central Conservatory and Columbia University in New York, Tan Dun has created world-premiere recordings of his opera "Marco Polo" and "Symphony 1997" (Heaven Earth Mankind), a large choral-orchestral work written to commemorate the occasion of the return of Hong Kong to China. Tan Dun's original score for "Crouching Tiger, Hidden Dragon" features performances by cellist Yo-Yo Ma, who was also soloist on "Symphony 1997."

For the BBC's live, 27-hour coverage of the arrival of the millennium around the world, Tan Dun created original music that appears on "A World Symphony for the Millennium." He composed a signature theme for the coverage and an elaborate suite that was heard throughout the live telecast around the world as viewers welcomed in the Millennium.

Tan Dun himself conducted the Sony Classical recording of "Symphony 1997" (Heaven Earth Mankind), performed live at the reunification ceremony in Hong Kong on July 1, 1997. In the fall of 1997, "Marco Polo" had its American debut at the New York City Opera. This highly original operatic treatment of the spiritual journey of the adventurer Marco Polo was commissioned by the Edinburgh Festival and premiered in 1996 at the Munich Biennale, with subsequent performances at the Holland and Hong Kong Festivals. The German magazine "Oper" named Tan Dun composer of the year for "Marco Polo."

Among many international awards he has received, Tan Dun was named one of the Musicians of the Year (1997) by the "New York Times" and was selected by Toru Takemitsu for the 1996 City of Toronto Glenn Gould Prize in Music and Communication. Tan Dun is currently the artistic director of the Tanglewood Contemporary Festival and the artistic director of the 2000 Festival for Barbican Centre London.

## ABOUT THE PRODUCTION COMPANIES

**SONY PICTURES CLASSICS** continues to be the leading distributor of independent films. Among the company's recent releases are Woody Allen's "Sweet and Lowdown," which received two Academy Award nominations (Best Actor—Sean Penn, Best Supporting Actress—Samantha Morton); Tom Twyker's "Run Lola Run," one of the highest-grossing foreign language films of the decade; and the 1999 Academy Award winner for Best Foreign Film, Pedro Almodovar's "All About My Mother." Current releases include Bruno Barreto's "Bossa Nova," starring Amy Irving, and Takeshi Kitano's "Kikujiro." The company's slate in 1998 and 1999 included such hits as David Mamet's "The Spanish Prisoner," produced by Jean Doumanian; the film was one of the highest grossing specialized releases of 1998. Other titles included "The Opposite of Sex," the critically acclaimed comedy which garnered the New York Film Critics Circle award for Lisa Kudrow (Best Supporting Actress); "Dancing at Lughnasa," starring Meryl Streep; "Central Station" (for which Fernanda Montenegro received a Golden Globe nomination and an Academy Award nomination for Best Actress); and "The Dreamlife of Angels" (winner of the 1998 Best Actress Award at the Cannes Film Festival).

**GOOD MACHINE INTERNATIONAL** (GMI) was founded at the 1997 Venice Film Festival as a film sales, marketing, and financing entity. In addition to films produced and acquired by production company Good Machine, Inc., GMI maintains an ongoing relationship with USA Films as the latter's exclusive foreign sales agent while also working on films separately with Universal Pictures, New Line Cinema, Columbia Pictures, Miramax Films, Sony Pictures Classics, and Fine Line Features, among others. GMI is now prepping four projects that are scheduled to begin production this year. Among them are Todd Solondz's untitled new

film with New Line Cinema, USA's "Flora Plum" from "Sixth Sense" producer Barry Mendel and director Jodie Foster, starring Claire Danes and Russell Crowe, "The Barber Movie" from Joel and Ethan Coen, and "Y Tu Mama Tambien," the next feature from Alfonso Cuaron.

**COLUMBIA PICTURES FILM PRODUCTION ASIA** was created in 1998 by Sony Pictures Entertainment to produce films for Asian audiences and represents the newest in a line of local language production divisions SPE has established around the globe, including the U.K., Brazil, and Germany. In the two years since its formation, the company has moved quickly to establish itself as an important player in the region with Zhang Yimou's Golden Lion award–winning "Not One Less," Hong Kong action master Tsui Hark's "Time and Tide," Ang Lee's "Crouching Tiger, Hidden Dragon," and the company's second film with Zhang, "The Road Home," which was awarded the Silver Bear at the 2000 Berlin International Film Festival. Headquartered in Hong Kong and with offices in China and Taiwan, Columbia Pictures Film Production Asia currently has a full slate of projects in development with talent from across the region.

# CREDITS

## CAST

Li Mu Bai . . . . . . . . . . . . . . . . . . . . CHOW YUN FAT
Yu Shu Lien . . . . . . . . . . . . . . . MICHELLE YEOH
Jen . . . . . . . . . . . . . . . . . . . . . . . . . . . ZHANG ZI YI
Lo . . . . . . . . . . . . . . . . . . . . . . . . . . . CHANG CHEN
Sir Te . . . . . . . . . . . . . . . . . . . . . . . LUNG SIHUNG
Jade Fox. . . . . . . . . . . . . . . . . . . . CHENG PEI PEI
Governor Yu . . . . . . . . . . . . . . . . . . . LI FA ZENG
Bo . . . . . . . . . . . . . . . . . . . . . . . . . . . . . GAO XIAN
Madam Yu . . . . . . . . . . . . . . . . . . . . . . . . HAI YAN
Tsai . . . . . . . . . . . . . . . . . . . . . . . . WANG DE MING
May . . . . . . . . . . . . . . . . . . . . . . . . . . . . . . . . LI LI
Auntie Wu . . . . . . . . . . . . . . . . . . HUANG SU YING
De Lu. . . . . . . . . . . . . . . . . . . . . ZHANG JIN TING
Maid . . . . . . . . . . . . . . . . . . . . . . . . . . . YANG RUI
Gou Jun Pei . . . . . . . . . . . . . . . . . . . . . . . LI KAI
Gou Jun Sihung . . . . . . . . . . . . . FENG JIAN HUA
Shop Owner . . . . . . . . . . . . . . . . . . . DU ZHEN XI
Captains . . . . . . . . . . . . . . . . . . . . XU CHENG LIN
                                       LIN FENG
Gangster A. . . . . . . . . . . . . . . WANG WEN SHENG
Gangster B . . . . . . . . . . . . . . . . . . . SONG DONG
Mi Biao . . . . . . . . . . . . . . . . . . . MA ZHONG XUAN
Flying Machete Chang . . . . . . . . . . LI BAO CHENG
Monk Jing. . . . . . . . . . . . . . . . . . . YANG YONG DE
Male Performer. . . . . . . . . . . . . ZHANG SHAO JUN
Female Performer . . . . . . . . . . . . . . . . . MA NING
Waiter . . . . . . . . . . . . . . . . . . . . . . ZHU JIAN MIN
Homeless Man . . . . . . . . . . . DON CHANG SHENG
Waitress . . . . . . . . . . . . . . . . . . . . . . . . . SHIH YI
Servant. . . . . . . . . . . . . . . . . . . . . . . . CHEN BIN
Nightman . . . . . . . . . . . . . . . . . CHANG SAO CHEN

## CREW

Line Producers . . . . . . . . . . . . . . . SHIA WAI SUM
                                       LIU ER DONG
Production Manager. . . . . . . . . . . . . . . . HELEN LI
Assistant Production
  Managers . . . . . . . . . . . . . . . . . PENG YU FONG
  LIU JIAN HUA, WANG JING HUA
  LI ZHAO, TSE CHI WAH
Production Coordinator. . . . . . . . PEH HUIE LING
First Assistant Directors . . . . . . . . LAI KAI KEUNG
                                       SYLVIA LIU
Second Assistant Directors. . . . . ZHANG JIN TING
  ZHOU YING YING, ZHU HONG BO
  XU CHENG LIN, TA BU SI
Script Supervisors . . . . . . . . . . . . . . SHERRIE LIU
                                       FENG YING
Assistant Script Supervisor. . . . . ZHENG SU JUAN

Art Department . . . . . . . . . . . . . . . . . EDDY WONG
  YANG ZHAN JIA, YANG XING ZHAN
  WANG JIAN QUO, ZHAO BIN
First Focus Puller. . . . . . . . . . . . . . . . KENNY LAM
Second Camera Assistant/Dollyman  LOUIS JONG
Crane Operator. . . . . . . . . . . . . . . . . JIMMY FOK
Loader . . . . . . . . . . . . . . . . . LEUNG WING HONG
Clapper. . . . . . . . . . . . . . . . . . . . . PATRICK HO
First Gaffer . . . . . . . . . . . . . . . . . LEE TAK SHING
Best Boy Electrician . . . . . SHUAN CHING CHUEN
Electricians. . . . . . . . . . . . . . . . . . NG MING HING
  LAM CHUN SHING, PUN HI HONG
Still Photographer. . . . . . . . . CHAN KAM CHUEN
Makeup Department. . . . . . . . . . . MAN YUN LING
  LIU JIAN PING, REN YI GONG
  LIU JING DONG, FAN YONG HAO
Hairdressing . . . . . . . . . . . . . . . CHAU SIU MUI
Wardrobe Department. . . . . . . . HSU SHU CHEN
  HUANG BAO RONG, WANG RONG
  ZHAO ZHI BIN, CHAI JUN, GU JIN HUA
Costume Assistants. . . . . . . . . . ZHENG YU JUAN
                                       CAO WU TONG
Property Department . . . . . . . . . . HUNG HIN FAT
  NG CHUNG WAI, FUNG SHU WING
  LI MING SHAN, LI BAO TAI
  WANG SONG BO, HO YI
Property Assistants . . . . . . . . . . . . . JI DA JIANG
  LI WEI ZHENG, TIAN CAI MING
  WANG CHENG SHENG, ZHANG BING
  SUN SUE CHUEN, ZHANG JUN FENG
Set Department. . . . . . . . . . . . . . . . JIANG QUAN
  HE YAN QING, TIAN ZHONG HE
  LI YI, WANG HE GEN, ZHANG QUAN
Sound Mixer. . . . . . . . . . . ANDREW PAUL KUNIN
Boom Operator. . . . . . . . . GEORGE HUEY LEONG
Sound Assistant . . . . . . . . . . . . . . . . . GAO YING
Interpreter . . . . . . . . . . . . ZHANG ZHENG ZHENG
Video Operator . . . . . . . . . . . . . . WANG HAI ZHI
Production Accountant. . . . . . . . . . . JOYCE HSIEH
Location Accountant. . . . . . . . . . FAN MEI RONG
Accountants in Hong Kong . . . . . . . . CARME LEE
                                       ANGELA FUNG
Assistant to Mr. Lee . . . . . . . . . . DAVID  L. S. LEE
Assistant to Mr. Kong . . . . . . . . . . . ANNA LEUNG
Assistant to Mr. Hsu . . . . . . . . CHEN CHING WEI
Assistant to Mr. Chow . . . . . . . MICHAEL SKORIC
Assistant to Ms. Yeoh . . . . . . . CHENG LING YING
Assistant to Mr. Schamus . . . . . . . . . . JAWAL NGA
Secretary . . . . . . . . . . . . . . . . . . . MA CHUN YE

## MARTIAL ARTS DEPARTMENT

Assistant Martial
  Arts Coordinators . . . . . . . . . . KU HUEN CHIU
                                       WONG KIM WAI

Martial Arts Stunts . . . . . . . . . . . CHAN SIU WAH
  CHAN FONG TAI, FUNG WAI LUN
  LAM CHI TAI, WONG WAI FAI,
  KOU ZHAN WEN, HE GUAN LIANG
  LIN FENG, GAO YUN LIANG, JIN CHUAN ZE
  ZHANG JIN, NING JUN, CHEN HU
  LIU HONG LIN, LI FENG MEI
Set Production Assistants. . . . . ZHANG ZENG HE
  SHI DONG SHAN, ZHANG HAI DONG
  WANG LU, ZHANG KAI
  SUN ZHEN WANG, WANG FENG PU
  LI JIE, DU JIN CHUN
  SUN YONG, ZHANG REN JUN
  NIU WEI, WANG LI MIN
  SHAN ZHAN BIAO
  DONG SHENG LIANG
  JIA LI JUN, CAO GAI MING
  ZHANG JIA LIANG, WANG HUA JIANG
Production Assistants. . . . . . . . . . SUN LIAN YU
  WU LIN HAN, JI TONG SHUN
  WANG GUO LIN, HAO SI
  ZHAO JUN JIE, XU FENG
  TIAN YONG SHENG, LI KAI
  ZHU HONG JUN, YU LEI
  LI ZHEN DUO, BAI HONG QUN
Staff Members. . . . . . . . . . . . . . . . . . . . GU WEI
  SUN SHAO YUAN, ZHAO GUO LI
  WANG TAO, ZHANG XIAN QIAN

## SECOND UNIT

Second Unit Cameraman . . . . . . . . CHOI SUNG FAI
Second Unit Focus Puller . . . . . . . . JIMMY KWOK
Second Unit Clapper/loader . . . LAU WAI KWAN
Video Operator. . . . . . . . . . . . . . . . . . . TANG PIN
Underwater Photography  MARC ROBERT SPICER
Second Unit Gaffer . . . . . . . . . . LAM CHUN WAN
Second Unit electrician. . . . . . . LAW WING TONG
Camera Grips. . . . . . . . . . . . . . . . . . . . . HAI TAO
                                       BAO FENG XIANG
Lighting Grips . . . . . . . . . . . . . . . . . . BA TE, HA SI
                                       HONG HAI, GAO YUN
Unit Publicists. . . . . . TESSA LAU, WANG & GLUCK

## POST PRODUCTION

First Assistant Editor. . . . . . . . . . . . TIM STREETO
Second Assistant Editor. . . . . . . . SHELBY SIEGEL
Conform Assistant . . . . . . . . . DREW BUCKLAND
Post Production Supervisor . . . . . JEFF ROBINSON
Post Production Assistant . . . . ANGELA BELLISIO
Supervising Sound Editor . . . . . EUGENE GEARTY
Sound Effects Editors. . . . . . . . . . . . BLAKE LEYH
  "JENNIFER RALSTON, M.P.S.E."
Dialogue Editors. . . . . . . . . . . LEWIS GOLDSTEIN
                                       PAUL URMSON

Re-Recording Mixer . . . . . . . . . . . . REILLY STEELE
ADR Editors. . . . . . . . . . . . . . . . . . KENTON JAKUB
GINA ALFANO
HAL LEVINSOHN M.P.S.E.
LISA J. LEVINE
ADR Supervisor . . . . . . . . . . . . . . . . . . JEAN TSIEN
Foley Editor. . . . . . . . . . . . . . . . . . . . BEN CHEAH
"JENNIFER RALSTON, M.P.S.E."
Foley Artist . . . . . . . . . . . . . . . MARKO COSTANZO
Foley Engineer. . . . . . . . . . . . . . . . GEORGE LARA
Assistant Sound Editors. . . . . . . . . IGOR NIKOLIC
BETTY TENG
Apprentice Sound Editors . . . . . HEATHER GROSS
ALEX SOTO
Intern . . . . . . . . . . . . . . . . . . CHAD BIRMINGHAM
Technical Equipment Supplied and
Serviced by . . . . . SALON FILMS HONG KONG
Special Visual Effects. . . . . . . . MVFX, Los Angeles
Visual Effects Supervisor. . . . . . . ROB HODGSON
Visual Effects Producer JONATHAN F. STYRLUND
Production Coordinator . . MATT "45" MAGNOLIA
Compositors. . . . . . . . . . . . . . . TRAVIS BAUMANN
MARY S. LEITZ
ANTHONY "ANTMAN" MABIN
JOHN SASAKI
3D Supervisor. . . . . . . . . . . JOHN "DJ" DesJARDIN
3D Artists. . . . . . . . . . . . . . . . . . ROBERT CHAPIN
JOHN CASSELLA, JR., BILL DIETRICH
MARK SHOAF, DANIEL SUNWOO
JENNIFER BEHNKE, DEVORAH PETTY
Paint/Roto Artist . . . . . . . . . GILBERT GONZALES
Editor. . . . . . . . . . . . . . . . . . . . . PATRICK BALLIN
General Manager. . . . . . . . . . . . . . . . . DON FLY
Bidding Producer. . . . . . . . . . . . . . . ROD PARK
Technical Assistants . . . . . . . . . . . NICOLLE GRAY,
DAVID LEE, SHELDON RAMONES
Runner. . . . . . . . . . . . . . . . . . . . . SEAN WHITE

Wire Removal and Digital Effects
ASIA LEGEND LIMITED, Hong Kong

Production Manager. . . . . . . . . . . . . . . . . . LEO LO
Production Organizer. . . . . . . . . . . BESSIE CHEUK
Production Supervisor . . . . . . . . . . MARCO POON
CGI Artists . . . . . . . MARCO POON, ANGIE CHAN
Speed Variation in Charge . . . . . . . . ANGIE CHAN
Chief Wire Removal Artist . . . . TOMMY CHEUNG
Wire Removal Artists . . . . . . . ROY NG, BERRY HO
MELISSA LO, HYDE CHOW, KENT KEI
ERICA YU, WINNIE HUNG, JESSICA LEUNG
Good Machine International/Executive in
Charge of Production . . . . . . . . KELLY MILLER
Legal Services
Provided by SCHRECK ROSE & DAPELLO LLP

Production Financing
Provided by. . . . . . . NATEXIS BANQUE –BFCE
Color Timer. . . . . . . . . . . . . . . . . . . . FRED HEID

Completion Guaranty Provided through
Cinema Completions International, Inc.

Color by . . . . . . . . . . . . . . . . . . . . TECHNICOLOR®
Dailies Advisor . . . . . . . . . . . . . . . JOE VIOLANTE
Dailies . . . . . . . . . . . . . MANHATTAN TRANSFER
Dolby Sound Consultant . . . . . . . JAMES ZIEGLER
Editing Facilities by. . . . . . . . . . . GOOD EDIT, INC
Insurance . . . . . . . . . . . . SPEARE AND COMPANY
TOM APLER
Negative Cutter . . . STAN AND PATRICIA SZTABA
WORLD CINEVISION SERVICE
Payroll Service . . . . ENTERTAINMENT PARTNERS
Post Production Sound. . . . . . . . . . . . . . C5, INC
Post Production Sound Service SOUND ONE CORP.
Titles and End
Credits by ASIA LEGEND LIMITED, Hong Kong
Video Dailies by MANHATTAN TRANSFER/EDIT
Colorist. . . . . . . . . . . . . . . . . . . PANKAJ BAJPAI
Audio Layback
by . . . . . MANHATTAN AUDIO PLAYGROUND
Video Dailies Supervision
by . . . . . . . POST PRODUCTION PLAYGROUND
AKI OHNUKI
Music Composed and Conducted by . . . TAN DUN
Scoring Producers. . . . . . . . . . . . . . . . TAN DUN
STEVEN EPSTEIN
Scoring Mixer. . . . . . . . . . . . . . . RICHARD KING
Technical Supervisor . . . . . . . . . . . . MARK BETTS
Assistant Engineers . . . . . . . . . . . LU XIAO XING
XU GUO QING
Music Production PARNASSUS PRODUCTIONS INC.
EMMY TU, PEI WEN ZHAO
Cello Solos. . . . . . . . . . . . . . . . . . . . YO-YO MA
Erhu Solo. . . . . . . . . . . . . . . . . . MA XIAO HUI
Bawu and Dizi Solo . . . . . . . . . . TANG JUN QIAO
Percussion Solo . . . . . . . . . . . . . . DAVID COSSIN
Music Performed
by. . . . . SHANGHAI SYMPHONY ORCHESTRA
"CHEN XIE YANG, CONDUCTOR"
SHANGHAI NATIONAL ORCHESTRA
SHANGHAI PERCUSSION ENSEMBLE
Electronic Programming . . . . . . . . . . . . TAN DUN
YUAN LIN CHEN
Music Recorded at . . . SHANGHAI RADIO FILM &
TV BUREAU TECHNICAL CENTER

CARAVAN BELLS ON THE SILK ROAD
Traditional Xinjiang Folk Song
Arranged by. . . . . . . . . . . . . . . . . . . NING YONY

Performed by. . . . . . . . . . . . . . . . . . . . . LIU BO
Published by. . . CHINA RECORD CORPORATION,
SHANGHAI, 1994

A LOVE BEFORE TIME
Music composed by. . . . . . . JORGE CALANDRELLI
TAN DUN
Lyrics by . . . . . . . . . . . . . . . . JAMES SCHAMUS
Translation by . . . . . . . . . . . . . . . . ELAINE CHOW
Produced by . . . . . . . . . . . . JORGE CALANDRELLI
Performed by . . . . . . . . . . . . . . . . . . COCO LEE
Featuring cello solo by . . . . . . . . . . . . . . YO-YO MA

Coco Lee appears courtesy of Sony Music
Entertainment (Holland) B.V.

Original Motion Picture Soundtrack
Available on SONY CLASSICAL

The producers wish to thank the following:
Beijing Film Studio
China Xinjiang Air Company
Beijing Liangxing Hotel
Beijing Ziyu Hotel
Beijing Continental Hotel
Hebei Cangyanshan Scenery Administration Office
Huangshang Feicui Valley Travel Service
Huangshan Jingyi Traveling Development
Corporation
Hongcun and Nanping Scenery Administration
Office
"China Bamboo Sea" Scenery Association of Anji,
Zhejiang Province
"China Bamboo Village" of Anji, Zhejiang Province
Chengde Bureau of Cultural Relics and Parks
Chengde Puning Mountain Villa
Xinjiang Branch of Guangdong Today Group
Corporation Ltd.
The Local Government of The Bai Seng Tang
District in Karamayi City
Chung Ar Chen
Bennett Pozil
Anthony Bregman
Norman Gay
Bill Nisselson
Phil Stockton
Cinema Completions International Inc.